W9-AUS-002

[100 THINGS WE'VE LOST TO THE INTERNET]

PAMELA PAUL

CROWN
NEW YORK

Published in the United States by Crown, an imprint of Random House, a division of Penguin Random House LLC, New York.

CROWN and the Crown colophon are registered trademarks of Penguin Random House LLC.

All illustrations by Nishant Choksi.

Library of Congress Cataloging-in-Publication Data
Names: Paul, Pamela, author.
Title: 100 things we've lost to the internet / Pamela Paul.
Other titles: One hundred things we have lost to the internet
Description: New York: Crown, [2021]
Identifiers: LCCN 2021023988 (print) | LCCN 2021023989
(ebook) | ISBN 9780593136775 (hardcover) |
ISBN 9780593136782 (ebook)
Subjects: LCSH: Interpersonal relations. | Internet—
Social aspects.
Classification: LCC HM1111.P37 2021 (print) |
LCC HM1111 (ebook) | DDC 302.23/1—dc23
LC record available at https://lccn.loc.gov/2021023988
LC ebook record available at https://lccn.loc.gov/2021023989

PRINTED IN THE UNITED STATES OF AMERICA ON ACID-FREE PAPER

crownpublishing.com

2 4 6 8 9 7 5 3 1

First Edition

Book design by Elizabeth Rendfleisch

For M, B, Mr. T., T2 + Z, L, and O/T

"One morning you'll simply wake up and it will be over, before you've even realized. Lying still, eyes closed, ears pricked, trying to sense the flow of the morning air, you'll feel that something has changed from the night before, and you'll know that you've lost something, that something has been disappeared."

—Yoko Ogawa, *The Memory Police*

CONTENTS

100
THINGS
WE'VE LOST
TO THE
INTERNET

INTRODUCTION

The Internet has brought us so much—information, access, connection, entertainment, discovery, delight, engagement, enrichment, and, occasionally and for a select few, actual riches. But because nothing about progress is ever straightforward, just as it brought us these things, it has taken things away. Some of these lost things were immediately evident: the photo albums we once painstakingly assembled using those sticky corners that inevitably stuck on crooked; the CD collection alphabetized by genre that represented who we were at our core and what we hoped others would see in us; the way we used to rush to the mailbox in the hopes of a surprise postcard from a friend abroad.

Other things we sensed more slowly, well into the aftermath of their disappearance: things that were gone or as good as gone, so far had they drifted in character from their pre-Internet selves. Like the college reunion that no longer abounds in startling revelations about who ran off with the babysitter or who has aged well and who has let it all go. Or the kind of customer service you could get only in the Bloomingdale's shoe department, where you and the saleswoman would hunt down the right dress pump for Saturday night as if united in a shared mission. These vanishings—products, services, and practices that had hummed along with contented acceptance for as far back as we could remember—were wiped out in less than ten short years, before we could fully grok the implications. What happened? Where did *that* go? Wait, since *when*?

We are all well aware of the weighty effects of the Internet on democracy, on citizen participation and fair elections and government accountability, on the fate of small businesses and the lives of workers; we have gone through the repeated realization that every time the Internet swings the door wide open, the consequences are at once liberating and dire. We know too well the Internet's trickle-down effects on our daily existence, from the screen we tap rather than the button we press when we wake in the morning; from what we do upon rising from bed to what we worry about as we drift off at night; from the particulars of our commute and what happens once we get to work and how we gather as a family when we return home. The ways in which we negotiate the school day and the summer vacation. How we see ourselves and treat one another; how we grow up and how we grow old.

All this we know. Less remarked upon is what we used to do instead.

I started writing this book well before the coronavirus pandemic hit, already feeling the ways the Internet was navigating where my brain wandered, occasionally startled and at other times lulled by what didn't always feel like a choice, yet unaware how much deeper the quarantine would plunge me—like everyone else—into a world that was "online only." And thank goodness the Internet was there! It was, quite plainly, a lifeline, providing vital health and safety information, the ability to work from a remote location, and a semblance of connection when we were all forced to live apart. Just try to imagine what the pandemic would have been like without it. But the Internet also made us feel more keenly the losses of what we'd left behind in the physical "out there."

Even without that viral nudge, one by one, objects, concepts, habits, and ideals that used to matter to us have fallen, sometimes with little more than a whisper, into the Internet. It can be hard to retrieve what life looked like in the before. But take a moment to think back on something as unassuming as a Saturday morning, the slowness of lazing in bed quite certain you were missing nothing exciting, snuggling down under the blankets for yet another fifteen-minute snooze. You'd wake and stretch, relishing the quiet before anyone else got up, unimpeded by what was going on in other people's heads. The outside world remained a distant concern, something for you to engage with only when you turned on the radio or stepped out the front door. These days you may be scrolling through the thoughts and thoughtlessness of 1,500 people you barely know while still on the toilet, not even aware who else in your own house is awake and doing the exact same thing.

What does it mean when so much of our lives is filtered through a pixelated lens, and is it still possible to capture what it looks like in the old unmediated way? One paradox of the Internet is that while it has opened up the world to us, it has also made that world feel small. We've witnessed a rectangular screen reduce an exuberant class full of children to a grid of glassy-eyed six-year-olds only half-present for their exhausted, quarantined teacher, who no longer bounds into the room full of energy for circle time, smelling faintly of gardenias or chocolate chip cookies. We have seen the magnificent sight of a rocky New Zealand shore reduced to a desktop background. Spend a few hours surfing around online and the world can look petty, repetitive, and flat.

Online (where else?) people will lament the passing of certain pre-Internet passions. One ongoing meme involves citing things that no longer exist and would stump a twenty-year-old. These lists are themselves liked and favorited repeatedly, nostalgically, almost ecstatically: Dialing a rotary phone! DVD extras. CD-ROMs. In the spring of 2019, a popular discussion on Reddit asked, "What's something the Internet killed that you miss?" The responses included moving examples of small but significant relics from the recent past. The highest ranked was "Having a mental catalog of great jokes that most people hadn't heard." One person mourned the toppled primacy of specialized knowledge: "My dad says he misses having arguments with friends which could only be resolved by phoning whoever was most knowledgeable on a subject e.g. Did you know lightning travels upwards? No, it goes down! Let's phone your dad, he's a meteorologist." Another marked the death of shortwave radio: "I had so much fun trying to tune in stations all around the world and putting pins in my world map for all of the ones I managed . . . and you could also write to the stations with a report and get postcards and pennants and other swag from them," he wrote. "I found my old shortwave radio a year or two ago (from Radio Shack—another thing I miss!), and you can still get some stuff, but the bands are dead for the most part. It's sad that magic is gone."

Is the magic gone? Or is only some of the magic gone while other forms of enchantment—the entire Internet is indisputably a kind of magic—are gained? After all, these Redditors would not have had a forum in which to discuss their wistfulness over shortwave radio were it not for the almighty Internet. Without access to this space, they may not have found fellow shortwave radio devotees from around the world with whom to commiserate. That I'm-the-only-one feeling that so many of us have felt at one point or another can be dissipated in an instant by wandering into the right subthread or by entering the beginning of a question into Google only to see the rest of it filled in like a psychic describing your current predicament with uncanny accuracy. Other people are there too, tapping in their embarrassing questions and darkest fears—others just like you.

As for the losses, to many of our pre-Internet ways we can say farewell and good riddance! Does anyone miss having to drive to three different hardware stores to find the right battery for a flashlight? Or arguing with a spouse over the name of the movie Joe Pantoliano played that guy in last summer? Hunting through the yellow pages for the GE customer service number only to find that it's already been changed? Wishing you could get back in touch with someone from childhood and having no clue where to start? Wanting to make something tasty with the wilting spinach and tiny heel of cheese in your fridge but not finding a decent recipe in the three oily cookbooks on your shelf? No one misses any of those pre-Internet hassles.

But other losses sting.

Now is the point at which, like anyone having a conversation around technology, I am forced to acknowledge, "I am not a Luddite." The Internet doesn't like people who quibble with the Internet, and any form of criticism can be taken as foot-dragging denial or starry-eyed romanticism, pathetic nostalgia or old fogeyism. To hesitate but for a moment is to bury your head in the sand and spurn the inevitability of the great march forward. I must assure you that I'm not unreasonably paranoid or hysterical about privacy or data, or the private sector's motives in collecting that private data, and that only part of me longs to live in a nineteenth-century cottage in the countryside, greeting neighbors by name as I pluck vine-ripened tomatoes from my garden and plan a weeklong re-thatching of the roof, which I detail each evening in a leather-bound journal by candlelight.

We all have our things. The things that I wildly appreciate online (mostly free returns and easy answers to basic questions) will not be the same as what others most value, and my keenly felt losses may not be the same as those of other people. We all have our own set of what we pine for—the fishing spot nobody else knew about, the September doorstop issue of *Vogue*, the longtime poker game member lost to online gambling, the pleasure of sitting down at a restaurant and opening up the menu not knowing what you and your companion would find. My own grievances reflect my experience as a Gen Xer, the worries of a journalist in a field under siege, the priorities of a reader for whom tucking a bookmark between pages is a cherished ritual, and the hopes and anxieties of a mother of three in New York. I've stood by as "my" things have been left behind and marvel that younger people will never know them, much the same way my dad once mourned the days-of-yore pleasure of stickball in the streets of Brooklyn, a ritual that seemed to me stuck in sepia dullness.

This is a book about our losses—the things we achingly miss, the things we hardly knew existed, the things to which we can give a hard adios—and about what their absence might mean. Some we are already beginning to lose sight of as the recent past gathers dust balls with increasing speed. Here we pause to document and delight in these recollections, turning them around in our collective minds to admire or mourn or celebrate, to push back against the possibility that the memories, too, may soon disappear.

BOREDOM

Remember boredom? The way it would hang over you when you were stuck in traffic and there was nothing decent on the radio and time dripped by? You'd be trapped in line at the supermarket, your eyes glazed after having read each headline on every tabloid wilting by the Doublemint gum, twice. You'd be waiting for your roommate to show up for dinner, having plotted your meal from hors d'oeuvres to dessert twenty minutes ago, or languishing at the doctor's office with nothing but mottled old copies of *Reader's Digest* on offer. Boredom was available just about everywhere. Nothing to do, nothing to divert or distract you during what should have been precious free moments amid the frantic hours of so much else to get done. You realize you could have brought a book, and why the hell didn't you?

But we have solved this because there is no more boredom. There are no empty moments and the mere thought of it—and who has time to think about it?—seems absurd.

Not so long ago, Motorola coined the term "micro-boredom" to describe those scattered, small moments that might bedevil us but could be solved in an instant by the smartphone—no sooner was the term coined than the problem was eliminated. The slightest void can be filled with a thumb to the screen: apps, clips, posts, links, the next bout of unfettered binge-watching all at the ready. Any number of friends, acquaintances, colleagues, Facebook "friends," Words with Friends players, or chat group participants is on your wrist or in your pocket, set to engage.

A novelist acquaintance told me how chagrined she was by her capacity to procrastinate online in lieu of working on her next book. (Join us, do.) After spending an entire afternoon on Instagram, to the point where she'd seen every last post on her timeline, she was gripped by the sudden fear that one day she'd arrive at a point where there was nothing more to see. The message on her phone would simply say, "That's it. You're done. You've reached the end of the Internet." I mentioned this to one of my children and he said, "That joke is everywhere."

Kids grow up with an ever-present escape valve, like a built-in ejector seat from any unwanted situation. They never really have to be there if they don't want to be, and neither do the adults. The second most common reason people use Facebook, by their own admission, is to alleviate boredom. My husband's standard line when I ask him what he thought of a particular lecture or show has been to say derisively when it had zero interest for him, "I went to SeaWorld," but now he or anyone else can actually—rather than metaphorically—go to SeaWorld, or at least some live-cam simulacrum, at any time. Tuning out no longer means spacing out; it means tuning in to something else.

People used to accept that much of life was boring. The word "boredom" didn't even emerge until the mid-nineteenth century, in part because it was nothing to be remarked upon. Life was boredom and boredom was life, whether it descended in the wheat field or at the spinning wheel. Memoirs of pre-twenty-first-century existence are rife with long stretches of tedium, no matter how much money you had to fritter away. When not idling in drawing rooms, the leisure class took aimless walks down empty footpaths and gazed at trees. They went motoring and gazed at more trees. Those who had to work for a living had it harder. Agricultural and industrial and office jobs were often mind-numbing; few people were looking to be fulfilled or engaged by paid labor. Children got used to the idea from an early age, left unattended with nothing to distract them other than maybe a bookshelf or tree branch.

Only a few short decades ago, during the lost age of underparenting, grown-ups thought a certain amount of boredom was appropriate, even to be encouraged, because it forced kids to exercise their imagination and ingenuity. A little ennui would make a person less bored in the long run.

Nowadays, subjecting a child to inactivity is seen as a gross dereliction of parental duty; thus, the proliferation of extracurricular, after-school, on-top-of-everything-else opportunities and efforts to engage. But when not being überparented and micromanaged, kids are left to their own devices—their own digital devices, that is. Parents preparing for a long car ride or airplane trip are like army officers plotting a complicated land maneuver. Which movies to load onto the iPad? Should we start a new family-friendly podcast? Is this an okay time to let the kids play Fortnite until their brains melt into the back seat?

What did parents in the seventies do when kids were bored in the back? Nothing! They let them suck in gas fumes. Torture their siblings. And since it wasn't actually used for wearing, play with the seatbelt. If at any point you complained about being bored at home, you were really asking for it. "Go outside," your parents would roar, or worse, "Clean your room."

But it was only while lolling around the basement or backyard that you'd settle into the anesthetizing effects of boredom, and with that monotony, your brain would kick into action, attempting to compensate. You might notice the world around you, both the minute and the grand, at its natural pace, letting go of the need to relentlessly move on to the next new thing. Small observations would begin to emerge and coalesce into ideas. There's a reason people have their most exciting and original thoughts in the shower. Our minds start to wander and we follow. You have to turn off the input in order to generate output. But the input never stops.

THE PERIOD

s any punctuation mark less remarked on than the lowly period, the wearisome little dot whose job it is, essentially, to bring you to a full stop? Nobody talks about it. There is no literary tradition of fiery opinions pro or con. Compared with the spirited grammatical infighting over the semicolon, the Oxford comma, or the overused em dash, the period and its impending obsolescence elicit nothing more than a half-hearted yawn.

Yet there is much to recommend in the plain old period. It is straightforward and decisive, yet also unassuming (with none of the wishy-washy of the parenthetical). The period does its work and moves on to the next sentence. And now it's done. Or as it is now written: Done

Online, the period is at best optional. On Twitter, you do not end a sentence with a period unless the intention is to look like you don't know what you're doing. In a text, a period seems at best stuffy, at worst absurd, and can bear an unintended gravity. Periods have come to mean something difficult, something bad. One recent linguistics study found that periods not only have grown altogether rare in short, informal text messages, but, in general, are mostly used to talk about weighty matters. Periods imply that someone is choosing their words carefully. Periods are for when you are called into a meeting with your boss and it's not to shoot the breeze. Periods mean someone is pretty darn unhappy on the other side of the screen. Periods age and date you and bring everyone down. "Only old people or troubled souls put periods at the end of every message," writes Victoria Turk in her modern etiquette guide, *Kill Reply All*.

The period can feel so emphatic as to sound sarcastic, the Internet's version of "puh-leeze," and "no, thank you" and "srsly" rolled into one tiny dot, a tendency that emerged early on in the digital age and strengthened over time. By 2009, Gretchen McCulloch, an "Internet linguist," notes, one user defined the period as "the new cool way to emphasize (usually moody-ass) sarcasm." It can even come across as passive-aggressive, a tendency McCulloch dates to 2013.

Part of the period's problem is not about what it is, but about what it fails to be: an exclamation point. No longer restricted to bursts of childlike enthusiasm or the occasional and extraordinary emphasis, exclamation marks now convey warmth and sincerity. So much so that when the exclamation is absent, you can't help feeling disappointed. *He must not have liked my idea,* you find yourself thinking when the email just says "Thanks" or "Cool."

And that's why the exclamation point is everywhere. Everywhere! Gmail's auto response never offers you a mere "Thanks." Even without an AI assist, try writing an email without an exclamation point insinuating itself somewhere where a period used to do just fine. You'll sound like a jerk. The recipient is bound to read it and think, "Did I do something wrong?" Against your better instincts, against everything you learned in college, against what you were told to do in professional communications, especially if you're a woman, you're going to write "Thanks!" Or even "Thanks!!" Not to do so now bears a marked lack of good will. If you have a problem with that, you can employ a Gmail extension called Emotional Labor, which helps those clinging to their periods "brighten up" the tone of their email—mostly by adding exclamation points.

Oh, but it's a slippery slope. You find yourself questioning each period. You find you are debating whether two or three exclamation marks in a given response are best. One day you wake up and realize you are using emojis without irony. You are texting kisses to your kids and mulling over which color heart goes with which interoffice communiqué and whether it's weird to wink electronically at your supervisor. You've learned not to use ellipses at the end of every sentence. You may be middle-aged, but you are ending emails with eye rolls. And then in a spurt of self-consciousness, firing off a quick follow-up 😭.

THE KNOW-IT-ALL

B ack before we all carried the Internet around in our pocket, not knowing the answer to something—even something inconsequential—could drive a person bananas. It was always the most trivial thing, too. Trying to recall the name of the guy who first traversed the Arctic by foot, what in fact happened when Andrew Johnson was impeached, what is our state flower, anyway; this sort of thing could consume hours, especially when you knew that you knew the answer. All kinds of information, memories, ideas, story lines, and factoids were elusive, most especially the one you were trying to remember when put on the spot. If you didn't know, but needed to know, you had to ask everyone you met: "Can I just ask you something first?" What the hell was the name of the book with the thing about octopuses in it? What was the name of the tasteless, untraceable poison at the center of that movie plot, the one whose name had "midnight" in it? Maybe it was a play. The endless, infuriating, depressing parade of things you once knew, didn't know anymore, or never knew at all.

Within this vague and ignorant fog of the recent past, acquiring and retaining information was a feat. Some people got it through a first-class education and others were born with a hardy memory and others just had the knack for amassing scraps of data that other people didn't bother to pick up. The decade-long Trivial Pursuit craze was based on the impossibility of retaining these myriad bits—who could possibly get all those answers right?

Back when most people didn't know the answer to everything, the few who did could be lightning rods. There was that annoying person in your senior seminar who always interjected. The boyfriend who always had a lecture at the ready. The ever-the-expert colleague who just had to point out the actual facts of the matter or the surprising backstory, fishing choice bits of knowledge out of his personal treasure trove of insight and acumen. The one who always knew better. That guy.

He shall bother you no longer. Everyone these days has constant access to his "special" information. The inside stories get out, and surprising data points pollinate. The most beguiling urban myths have no time to take hold before they're snoped away. We can all fact-check now. (Though of course, this does nothing to prevent people from thinking they know things even when they don't, or deter people who claim to "know" things inside what one might gently call alternate realities.) Every moment of every day, people are seeking answers and finding them. Google processes more than 40,000 search queries worldwide per second, adding up to 1.2 trillion searches a year.

This makes knowing things not so special. When someone exults, "I actually *knew* that!"—meaning "I didn't have to look online"—does it even matter? Only I can award myself bonus points when I get through a grueling mental process like trying to remember who sung the theme song of the movie *Flashdance* ("That singer, Cara. Cara something . . . Cara Delevingne. No, duh, what is wrong with me . . . Cara Ireland?" and the final exaltation of "Irene Cara! Yes!") without going to the Internet for assistance. Yet it's so unusual I am tempted to relay each painstaking and pointless factoid win to another person to be commended for it.

Kids used to think that parents knew everything because even if they didn't, they'd make up some plausible answer on the spot or look it up in a book later that night and feign universal knowledge in the morning. Now kids witness their parents plunging into Google to find the names of Jupiter's moons or the precise scientific reason why oil floats on water. They learn early on that their parents don't know everything—but the Internet, oh, the Internet, does.

GETTING LOST

Getting lost—truly and hopelessly lost, which always happened late at night or when you were very hungry—is a bygone problem. But if you're of a certain age, you can well remember what it was like when you looked up and suddenly realized you had no clue where you were, panic surging from deep within your throat. It could be terrifying, especially if you were alone. It could also be terrifying when you were with your parents, each of them yelling about whose fault it was that you were still tooling down the same unmarked country road with no discernible landmarks, driving for forever only to discover that the restaurant where you were supposed to be thirty minutes ago was back in the opposite direction and then getting off the highway because you had to find somewhere, anywhere, but please-not-the-side-of-the-road, to pee and then being unable to find your way back on.

Must we get wistful over the loss of getting lost?

After all, it's nice to head in the right direction. We go

where we mean to go because the GPS and Google Maps know our precise destination and have shared our location with our loved ones. Without a doubt, knowing where you are and always having a means to get there have made life more efficient and less stressful. You don't have to write down the directions and then prop the marked-up sheet of paper on the passenger seat, or stop at the local AAA office to get a map or, better yet, a TripTik, or hunt down a pay phone to call for a rescue. You don't have to comb through the disorder of the bookstore's map section for the least rumpled copy of Western Massachusetts.

In this newfound world, place knowledge or a good sense of direction are no longer attributes to cultivate. You can no longer boast about knowing the best subway route or having hometown knowledge of weekend train construction like it's a rare achievement. Who cares if you can make your way around the West Village without a map or that you mastered the Thomas Guide in driver's ed?

Sure, we may run into occasional trouble. Uber sometimes tries to pick you up somewhere you're not. Google Maps isn't infallible. We can still get lost, and the kids get to observe vicious three-way fights between Mom, Dad, and Siri. Mapping apps have optimized new ways to get from A to B that often forgo the major routes and thoroughfares so that the paths people are led down aren't lined with the expected rest stops and road signs. You may be following directions and wind up on a twisty, disused road that feels all wrong. Formerly quiet residential streets are filled with late-night Lyfts hauling drunken teenagers.

Perhaps part of you misses, just a tiny bit, having someone else to blame for getting lost on the occasions when it still occurs. You can't say you misplaced or misread the directions or that someone must have written them down wrong. It was your fault. There's no wiseass at the gas station insisting you take a hard left, which maybe he did on purpose because he was secretly stoned or he didn't like your face. Now there is only the iPhone with its anodyne, computer-generated voice to blame if you misread the map or clicked on "Avoid highways" by mistake. Tell Siri she can go to hell all you want; she doesn't care.

With your trajectory always optimized, you also, inevitably, lose the alternate route, the surprise detours, and something much more intangible but perhaps the most beguiling and difficult to recover: the ability to lose yourself. If one of the worst parts of travel is getting lost, it can also be one of the best. It's in those lost moments that we succumb to chance and make our own discoveries. We no longer experience that terrifying and liberating exhilaration of not knowing, of not having the coordinates or indeed any clue where exactly on this giant lonely planet we are, and how we fit into it. Occasionally we will briefly lose and then regain our signal—and in those rare instances, we can recapture the thrill of at last being found.

5

LOSING YOUR TICKET

It had to happen to all of us, it seemed, at least once, though you'd swear after that first time that it would never happen again. You'd be running late to the airport, going over your mental checklist: bags, packed; suitcase, labeled; traveler's checks, in hand; and yes, you remembered your passport. Only then, just as your taxi approached the terminal, would you realize, horror-struck, that you'd left your plane ticket at home. Tickets: They were forgotten, lost, left behind, slipped out of your wallet and stuck to the back of something else, never to be recovered. You'd forget your tickets to tonight's show at the office, the image of the envelope tucked into the first compartment of your standing file rack, mocking you in your mind's eye. You'd have no idea what the hell you did with your monthly bus pass or the tickets to next week's game. You might have to fill out a form or spend hours on the phone with customer service, frantically trying to persuade someone that yes, you did buy a ticket and you were you. Occasionally, you wound up missing out on whatever you had planned.

It won't happen again. Your ticket—whether for the plane, the train, the show, the commute, or the World Series—is online and it's on your phone. You couldn't lose it if you tried. Nor can you lose your speech or tear it up dramatically in front of a crowd because that, too, is on your phone, nor can you throw your ticket in the trash and be done with an obligation you wish you'd never agreed to in the first place. It's hard to lose anything that exists as an image or block of text when it's in the link *and* the attachment, and is always backed up. You have the automated confirmation. You have the scannable QR code. You took a screenshot of it because you were smart with your smartphone. One of life's great and ever-repeated stressors is, blessedly, gone. Unless, of course, you lose your phone.

6

THE MEET-CUTE

How many couples do you know who actually met for the first time in an elevator? How many lonely singles have found their one and only at someone else's wedding, a wedding they almost didn't attend, their frenemy's wedding? How often would it happen that a woman tripped (albeit adorably) while running late (perhaps to meet the wrong person) and literally and metaphorically fell into destiny's arms? That kind of meet-cute was the stuff of rom-coms, and thus happened far more often in the movies than it ever did in real life.

Yet when it did take place down here on earth, the result was so shiny and enchanted, it was a story to be savored, to be shown off in a wedding announcement or in the class notes of an alumni magazine (RIP) and described over and over again at family dinners forevermore. Even if that first meet wasn't especially cute, the How I Met Your Mothers were still clues to the secret behind each couple and perhaps the closest you'd come to understanding the mystery of how one person you knew ended up tied to another one altogether, especially if the two seemed an odd or improbable match. It turns out he was the friend of her former roommate's ex-boyfriend who just happened to show up that night. They met in the produce aisle of Fairway or in that long line at the Balboa Theatre for that

Cannes favorite, which turned out to be terrible, and they had so much to complain about. Great potential would lie in these chance encounters; just hearing them, perhaps only during the wedding toast, would open up the possibility that if he met her or him this way, it could happen to you.

And so, despite its statistical unlikelihood, the meet-cute remained the stuff of daydreams and the basis of those encouraging words your best friend would console you with when you bawled on the bathroom floor during your interminable single years. You'll see, she'd say, spinning out the possibilities: You'll be sitting on a bus when a stranger will take the seat beside you, casually unlooping his backpack and placing it on his lap where you can just make out the title of his paperback (it's a good one). It could happen on the train. It could happen in the rain. (Maybe you're both Dr. Seuss fans.) You could start chatting each other up in a café in the days before everyone had coffee with their phone or laptop (try to imagine what kind of weirdo in the eighties would haul a typewriter to the local Starbucks). The I-see-you-over-there on the subway was so rife with possibility that it spawned an entire genre of local classified ad: the missed connection, a joy to readers of alternative weekly magazines (RIP).

Then it all migrated online. Craigslist, that 1.0 innovator, spawned the whole Internet of dating with its early digitization of newspaper missed connections. And personal ads. And everything else ads. Soon enough, the Internet was the elevator and the movie line and the department store and everywhere else; it was where we formed those connections instead.

And the Internet got very, very good at its job. It

matched an exciting number of early adopters and then mated new programs that matched people even better. It spawned Jdate and OkCupid and Match and Bumble and the remorseless Tinder, out-yentaing the yenta, leaving little to chance. Now we pick and choose our way to "the perfect match" according to preselected criteria that filter out people who may not share our religious beliefs or passion for gardening but who may have—we'll never know—made us deliriously happy. We are all following the formulas and obeying the algorithm set out by teams of unknown workers deep in Silicon Valley. In 2013, meeting online for heterosexual Americans eclipsed meeting through friends as the most popular way to find a romantic partner, a dominance that has continued apace. Today, seven in ten same-sex couples find each other this way. All told, nine out of ten couples in the *New York Times* wedding announcements met online, the stories of their first encounters basically free advertisements for competing dating services. The only question that remains for singles is which platform to choose.

7

BAD PHOTOS

In the days of the one-click Kodak, most pictures—
unflattering, off-center, accidental, overexposed, and everyone as red-eyed as vermin—were not worth keeping.
No one could figure out how to operate the focus. No one
knew when to turn off the flash, or how. Few people had
any sense of aesthetic. You could sift through a full roll of
fresh prints, their chemical scent almost wetting the air,
and not find a single picture that aimed somewhere less
ominous than the region directly below your chin.

And you never knew what you would get once the little
button was clicked. You had to wait to find out, often a
week or longer until twenty-four-hour photo shops, with
their bargain-basement development quality, were introduced. You'd head back to a Fotomat after dropping off the
little black plastic roll, full of hope, barely remembering
what was on there because film was precious and the roll
may have taken months to complete, especially if it was a

36 rather than a 24, only to open the envelope and yup: one blurred atrocity after another.

Things got worse during that crazed period in the nineties when every catered Sweet Sixteen party and wedding featured dozens of disposable Fuji cameras that somehow landed only in the hands of guests who couldn't take a single decent picture. You'd be tempted to throw a good number away, but more often you didn't, because film was expensive and throwing away photographs seemed like a vain and frivolous thing to do. Dare to snatch the paper from a friend's Polaroid as it scrolled out of the slot, convinced you'd been caught on film looking ridiculous, and you risked certain wrath.

Browsing through photo albums from this time is like encountering a dark period from an inexplicable and occasionally insane-looking past, one in which everyone cried at parties and scowled through reunions and looked miserable at their brother's Little League game. No one ever thought to bring a camera along on those rare occasions when you were looking your best. School pictures routinely documented the horror. Your braces. The uneven middle part. That mottled gray backdrop. Try as you might to hide the telltale 8 × 10 envelope from your parents—of course they'd ordered an overpriced set—they'd keep them anyway, as if out of spite. These once-a-year portraits were part of your childhood history! For the rest of adolescence, you'd flee from any adult wielding a camera.

From this angle, it's impossible to fathom the impending dominance of the selfie, a word that didn't even really exist in the United States until 2011. Who knew how much people would adore taking pictures of themselves? That teenagers, of all awkward and self-conscious creatures, could spend entire afternoons posing and perfecting. That seniors would love it so much, tour buses would make stops not for plain old photos of landscapes and landmarks but for selfies. That they would love it so much, entire "Instagram museums" would pop up purely for the purpose of taking selfies against wacky backgrounds; that in lieu of docents, staff members would stand by to help take photos of visitors posing from inside Instagram-ready installations. That hotels and restaurants would design bathroom lighting to enhance selfie potential. Yes, *bathroom* lighting. But the background is nonetheless secondary to the main attraction because in selfies, we all look our best.

8

FILING

Four standing files loom reproachfully in my garage, years after I've even attempted to rattle open one of their jam-prone metal tab closures. I haven't a clue what's in them anymore, but I also can't quite persuade myself that they're no longer necessary. They're my files, after all! One has always needed a place to hold the history of one's past and in alphabetical order: Artwork, by grade; camp letters; cards, birthday; cards, Valentine's Day; cards, other; insurance forms; house deed; medical records. Taking hold of one's papers was part of the work of adulthood; it meant requisitioning official paperwork from one's parents: birth certificate, childhood diplomas. Who knew when they might prove necessary?

The file cabinet was also part of every workspace and home office; there might be a maze of them in a storage room at the office or in your basement at home. For a writer, clips were essential. Any time one of your pieces appeared in a publication, you would go to the newsstand, buy several copies, and painstakingly tear out your article along the seam, using a razor if need be. You kept these clips filed by date and publication so that when you were approaching a new editor, you could send along a manila envelope of your clips with a cover letter. There were also the papers that documented your writing process on larger projects. Any writer worth his name in print had papers to file—primary research, first drafts, editorial notes—papers that someday might fetch a price from a library collection or university . . . should you be so lucky as to be asked to donate "your papers."

But there was nothing elevated about the act of putting all this in order, the dread act of filing. No matter what your profession, if you were ever an intern, an executive assistant, an office manager, a clerk, or a catalog manager, you had to file. You filed and filed until your thumbs wore down, and only after you'd climbed a few rungs on the corporate ladder could you hand the filing off to the person yet another rung down. Even then, you'd find yourself struggling to open a jammed drawer from time to time.

At my stepmother's promotional products agency, I spent entire summers putting away catalogs, which would arrive in yellow mailers each day. I'd find the appropriate cabinet, search for the appropriate hanging Pendaflex folder and then pull out the manila folder inside, pluck out Spring 1989 and replace it with Fall, everything alphabetized by title down to the third letter. I would then recenter the metal inserts, handwriting a label onto that tiny, perforated bit of paper, folding it just so and inserting it into the plastic tab only to see it slide out the other end. Finally, I would fight the drawer closed, sometimes with a hard kick to get it past its preferred sticking point.

Occasionally, in a nostalgic moment, I'll take the time to pry open one of those drawers in the garage and peer into my past. A visual remnant from the archives—a term paper for an anthropology class I'd forgotten about, a clipping from my hometown paper about the hurricane that knocked down our front tree—might catch my eye and I'll be transported back. The smell and weight of the paper, the vintage of the handwriting or the type of the dot-matrix print, all hurtle me back in time.

Who even prints these things out now? You don't just happen upon such things among the uniform folder icons in the cloud, opening and unfolding their contents gingerly or discovering something unexpected on the back. We can shut the door permanently on all of that.

9

EX-BOYFRIENDS

No matter how brief or unfortunate a relationship, you couldn't help but wonder—months and years later—what ever happened to your ex-boyfriend, the one you supported through med school, the one who always had to be right, the one who knew how to dance like no one else. Had he sulked for months when you split up, or had he gone out that night, gotten drunk, and gotten into bed with someone else? Did he start dating that girl from work you'd suspected he'd liked all along? Did it turn out he was gay? Unless you stayed in touch with his friends, you just didn't know. If you ever found out anything about his future endeavors, it was usually via a wedding announcement. Most of the time, that was for the best; you and he were over, and even if you were sulky or angry when it ended, it was best not to dwell.

There's no forgetting those exes anymore. Whether you still pine for them or couldn't care less, you can't put them out of your mind because they remain your friends on Facebook, or your friend of friends, or you're in the same industry and are inextricably LinkedIn. You cannot log off your ex-boyfriend when he pops up in searches or when you somehow find yourself scrolling around for him on a Friday night wondering *What the hell are you thinking?* as you do. You continue to traipse after each other on Instagram because it would seem like too much of a *thing* if you unfollowed. Collectively, you have 1,874 people in common.

He will be online where you can watch him, and he may be watching you, too, or, perhaps worse, he is not. Regardless, he is bound to show up when you least expect it, looking fit and well-adjusted, armed with a swanky new job and a sweet-looking girlfriend, which you will see in a flattering photo montage. You'll know everything about his upcoming nuptials down to the napkin pattern, and you will watch his perfect baby daughter as she is joyously welcomed into the world in a home birthing pool, surrounded by earthy music and a soulful doula, where she will thrive and look adorable for the foreseeable future against color-coordinated backgrounds. The Internet is for wallowing in one another's happiness.

Whether you call it low-buzz stalking, cyberstalking, or "creeping," people browse around the edges of their former intimates' lives where they inevitably learn much too much: Our former friends and loved ones can do inverted yoga poses; they have begun appreciating contemporary art; look at their fabulous house. Don't loiter too long on that post with your thumb or you may accidentally, horrifyingly, heart the image, alerting your ex to just how deep into his rabbit hole you've crawled. Or do: If you prefer to be the Evil Ex, you can partake in that insidious form of stalking called "aggressive liking," making sure to like every single post someone puts online, just to let him know you still care. Creepy.

People can try ghosting—disconnecting without breaking up or saying goodbye—or cloaking, a variant in which you not only stop responding to another person, but you also go dark altogether, blocking that person on all your apps. A single tick on WhatsApp will make clear you've been shut out. Or maybe your ex will "submarine" you, a gaslighting variation on ghosting in which someone cuts off all communication and then reappears months or even years later, acting as if nothing has happened. "Oh, hey!" But still, you see them choosing *not* to see you. This is not what we like to think of as moving on or getting over someone.

Teenagers are especially gifted at throwing their happiness around like a kitchen knife. They rub in bad breakups by tagging their exes in photos of themselves with their new beaus. Instagram calls this form of online bullying "betrayals." Teenagers call it normal.

For the newly or perpetually single, the Internet is fraught with painful TMI. It's bad enough to be a thirty-something woman wondering why that handsome divorcé isn't texting back after what felt like a promising first drink; now she can find out exactly. He said he wasn't ready for someone new? One look at his active profile on Match.com and his cover is blown. He just didn't like her.

10

BEING LATE

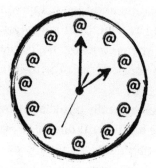

Wait, you're twenty minutes late? I had no idea. I mean, if anything, I'm grateful. I finally had a chance to read that crazy Nicolas Cage interview that blew up the Internet this morning or maybe it was yesterday morning, and I also saw the cat thing. You can tell I'm behind! But I did use the time to also catch up on email, or at least some of it. Hold on just one more minute, can I finish writing this one last one? Thanks. And thank you for being late! Maybe you can go ahead and catch up on your thing, too?

Nobody has to feel bad about being late anymore because waiting is "free" time, gained time, magic Internet time, and all of us can use it. Lateness is also rarely unexpected because we text from the train about the signal failure and ping again when we're two minutes away and let our next meeting know we're running just two minutes behind. "Np!" the person will reply. "I'm delayed too!" If our meeting is virtual, we don't ever have to leave the screen to accomplish this.

We are all late all the time even though we know the time better than ever before. Our alarm clocks never run out of batteries and nobody needs a watch unless it's a smart one, and the time is all synced together in the cloud, even when it leaps forward. In this curious world of constant time awareness, others' persistent lateness not only excuses our own, it helps us keep up with a clock that is always two steps ahead. Next time please be a little bit later.

11

BENIGN NEGLECT

Back in the days of Sugar Pops and roller skates, grown-ups had no clue where their kids were, who they were with, or what the hell they were up to, and that suited kids just fine. You walked to school on your own or with the kid down the street that Mom disapproved of. Maybe you each took your bikes and rode in the street against traffic together. She didn't need to know. The latchkey kids spent afternoons as they pleased; even those with stay-at-home parents didn't generally report in until dinner. Homework might be left undone, sugary snacks consumed. Bands of kids went out shoplifting in town and skateboarding in the school parking lot. The older ones toppled into cars carelessly driven by slightly older kids. That night, there was a party on the beach with a poorly maintained bonfire and three kegs, but all the parents knew was that you were going "out." They'd be asleep by the time you got home.

Somehow, kids grew up anyway. But any one of these casual practices of pre-Internet parenting now feels like an act of gross negligence. Internet parents don't need to wonder what the nine-month-old might be chewing on midway through the workday. They know precisely where she is and they also know whether she's giggling or crying or in mortal peril because at any moment, they can toggle over a tab to the nanny cam. They can text the sitter. They can look at the daycare's website and click on "playroom" and read the daily blog post about what was served for lunch. See if their little peanut got enough tummy time and finished her pear.

When she's five, parents can track her on her Gizmo, then her grown-up smartwatch, and then her own phone as she graduates from device to device, the Internet's way of marking a kid's milestones. On each gadget, parents can check where their eleven-year-old is, and who and what dumb or alarming stuff her friends are liking. There's no wondering what she's up to.

Nor is there a need to wonder about whether a thirteen-year-old will flunk Algebra I. With ClassDojo and the parent portal and the online grade book and the weekly email from each teacher, parents already know when to worry about what their son got on the music theory quiz. There shall be no nasty surprise when the report card comes home as an automated email sent to parent and child simultaneously. An unlucky fifteen-year-old won't ever have the chance to "forget" to bring home his report card (remember those heavy-paper rectangles, signed by a real person with a handwritten comment in pen?) or to manually alter a letter with Wite-Out or to pretend he hasn't received it.

His parents are already well aware. They know whether he played Fortnite for longer than his allotted forty-five minutes (yes), whether he's ever viewed online pornography (sorry), whether he has any friends at school (104, as of yesterday), whether he likes anyone or *likes* likes them (those texts!).

It's reassuring that if anything—god forbid—should ever happen to your sixth grader when he's walking home from school for the first time, you will know precisely where he is when whatever it is happens. It's reassuring that in those worst-case scenarios, you will at least be informed. But when kids today want to shake off their parents' watchful eyes, they know, too, exactly where to go—deeper into the Internet. They know how to hide in encrypted chambers, set up Finsta accounts, and only post to certain people and on platforms whose images disappear before parents can even contemplate peering in with their judgy eyes and faux-innocent questions. As they get older, kids turn the surveillance tools against their parents, who can watch all they want but won't see a thing.

12

THE DESIGNATED DRIVER

Unless you'd sworn off drinking, being named the designated driver could put a real damper on the evening. Who wanted sworn sobriety on the night of Alice and Joe's annual birthday blowout or on New Year's Eve? It was the subject of arguments and the grudging taking of turns, and someone always ended up sidelined as party pooper. Still, the knowledge that someone, perhaps even just that one person, would need to exercise self-control and get everyone home safe at the end of the night conferred a certain degree of restraint to an evening, no matter how debauched.

Now everyone can drink themselves silly. With Uber and Lyft ever ready, there's no need to argue over who will be the designated driver. Teenagers don't have to make humiliating calls home using their fake sober voice, pleading for their parents to fetch them because everyone left without them. Instead they can booze their way into oblivion and consume lord knows what other iffy intoxicants. They'll still have a chance to sneak in before their parents can see them stagger. They can conceal the cost of the evening through some sleight-of-hand maneuvering with Venmo.

But while no one especially celebrates a sixteen-year-old getting tanked on a Friday night, it's far preferable to hold back her sweaty hair while she vomits into your toilet at four A.M. than it is to get a dread call from the police about the latest teenage drunk-driving accident. Kids today think drunk driving is crazy. Many kids today think just plain driving at all is crazy.

13

THE PHONE CALL

Peple have always spent lots of time on the phone; the difference is that before, we spent it on actual phone calls. Imagine that.

The idea that the little device tucked into our pocket or clutched in our hands is called a "phone" at all seems odd when you consider what it really is: a computer. Does anyone in his right mind use an iPhone 12 Pro Max primarily to make calls? People would sooner use their phone to order pizza from Seamless than they would to call up the pizzeria. If the phone somehow rings, we usually pick it up only by accident—ack! I meant to press the red.

After the pandemic struck, people momentarily rediscovered that weird opportunity between texting and FaceTiming—"the phone call"—as if they'd never partaken in one before, certainly not intentionally or for fun, because these days, when someone asks you to chat, the baseline assumption is that the chat will be text based.

Speaking to someone by phone has evolved into "touching base" or "checking in," either of which is a brief intentional exchange, most often because it's too much to type in a text while wearing gloves or running. MIT's guru of Internet sociology Sherry Turkle calls this general tendency the "flight from conversation."

But we used to talk on the phone a lot, and people loved it. Kids wondered when the phone rang if it could possibly be for them. Teenagers adored talking all afternoon and into the night and pined for a princess phone or even a line of their own. For adults, talking on the phone was a quick way to alleviate the tedium of housework and parenthood and just plain nothing-to-do-ness. "Get off the phone!" family members would yell at one another. "Mom, she's been on the phone for over an hour!" "Are you *still* on the phone?" People called each other for no reason!

They also called each other for good reason. On the phone, things got *done*. Being "good on the phone" was a valued skill at work, worth boasting about in a job interview. In the workplace, the phones were constantly ringing. Entire jobs were built around the telephone—secretaries, customer service representatives, phone salespeople, operators; most of this turf now belongs to robots and bots. The laziest of employees knew that one of the most efficient ways to look busy was to wear a headset and bark into it at regular intervals. A power move was to have more than one line to yourself. Even if your job had nothing to do with telecommunications, you were likely on the phone—or trying to avoid being on it—most of the day.

Thank goodness that's over. Why, the post-phone generation might wonder? Well, for one thing, the phone always rang at the wrong time. Phone calls could be presumptuous and intrusive, forcing you to engage without preparation. Phone calls were rude. "What makes you think I can drop everything and talk to you right this instant?" you wanted to cry out when you were in the basement, emptying the mop bucket while the phone trilled belligerently upstairs.

Nowadays, people know you are far too busy on the phone with other things. Nobody dares interrupt your game, just as you arrive on Level 7 for the first time, with an unpremeditated call. No one rings when you're in the painstaking process of tapping out an important text or issuing instructions to Siri—unless it's a robocall or an emergency. They know to ping first, reaching out in a far less obtrusive manner. "Let's get one thing clear: Do not call unannounced unless someone's dying," explains modern etiquette guide Victoria Turk. The proper thing to do is text someone first or send a polite email in advance asking if it's okay to call, even if that call is merely to clarify an inscrutable text in recent group chat.

Frankly, texting is often better. You can read the message when you want to and answer when you choose. People for whom English isn't a first language can go at their own pace and can look up words online. Texting gets it all down in writing.

The rare in-depth phone call that somehow still occurs generally is taken by the person sitting directly behind you in an enclosed space. "I'm on the train," he'll begin, and then, just as you attempt a nap, launch into a heated monologue about his contractor's failure to show up that morning. Or someone will answer a blaring phone in an open-plan office and subject everyone to the details of their dental coverage. It may be that people are so unused to talking on the phone or so used to wearing headsets, they've lost all sense of volume control. We talk on the phone like we don't know how. It's possible we no longer do.

14

MEDICAL FORMS

The only thing worse than sitting down with a clipboard in the doctor's waiting room filling out five pages of forms, from the blow-by-blow history of every ailment and procedure you've ever had to the giving-away-all-your-privacy HIPAA sign-off, is tapping through eighteen screens on a padded tablet (do they worry people will throw them against the waiting room wall?), and then being asked to rate the experience on a scale of one to five stars. Or being required to fill in box after box in a slowly loading stream of online PDFs before you are even able to make a doctor appointment. Remember when you used to be able to call up a doctor and just find a time slot?

The less paper there is, the more questions they ask, and half of those questions seem geared toward the practice's marketing and data collection efforts rather than your personal healthcare. You would think that all this electronic data would mean better data sharing between doctors so that you didn't have to trouble yourself once again with every new specialist—alas, it does not. Systems still clash and insurance information gets lost and your test results somehow didn't get logged in to the database. Nobody can seem to upload the history. Would you mind emailing your other doctor with the request?

Once, as I was still laboring away on what felt like thirty

screens on a medical Etch A Sketch even after leaving the waiting room and beginning to undress in the doctor's office, all the while fielding questions from a nurse, I blurted out "I hate this thing!"

"All of us do," she replied, taking the offending tablet from my hands and flinging it onto a chair. "Don't bother." But sadly, at most doctors' offices, we must.

15

UNINHIBITEDNESS

How reassuring it was to know that however dreadful you were in the school play or however extravagantly you flubbed a presentation at work, you would never need to know how truly bad it was. After all, you would never see it yourself, and most people wouldn't tell you the truth even if you tried to coax it out of them. Over time, you could persuade yourself that maybe you weren't nearly as bad as your initial dark imaginings. In any case, you didn't have to dwell on it because those kinds of performative moments came and went and disappeared forever. Once, in fourth grade, a friend's rock star uncle showed up with a full camera crew to film her performance in *Annie*. Many people had never seen a video camera before, and the scene was viewed by the rest of Main Street School as the kind of extravagance that could only come with being a rock star. Who else would bother filming a fourth-grade performance? The answer today: everyone.

The stakes were lower before everything was a performance and all performances were uploaded to be shared and dissected for posterity. You no longer run out of the house looking like god knows what because you can see the disaster that is your hair on your phone (remember pocket mirrors?), and when you do—or worse, when someone else does—that ensures you'll never go outside looking like that again, or at least without worrying about it if you do. As I walk home through Times Square every night, it's hard to ignore the presence of hundreds of upheld cameras documenting every moment, taking in my own experience as they take in theirs. The thought of this spontaneous and unregulated surveillance system makes me hasten my pace, darting in and out of the camera's gaze. I find myself watching what I say to a fellow commuting colleague walking beside me, looking over my shoulder, well aware that someone—perhaps even my own phone!—may be inadvertently recording me. I don't want to unwillingly take part in someone else's livestream. You are always at risk of winding up on *Candid Camera*.

We've all had bouts of self-consciousness. Growing up, I, like nearly every teenager, feared everyone else was looking at me all the time, with the acute exception of those rare moments when I wanted to be seen. The reality, at once soothing and brutal, that nobody was actually looking at me during any of these moments, desired or not, was one of the hardest adult lessons to absorb. It may be that none of us has ever been entirely persuaded.

This has perhaps somewhat prepared us for a time when you never can be sure others aren't watching, so you best always be on your guard. You cannot will yourself to be invisible when you can readily be recorded on someone else's camera and see your words and image pasted online. Whereas the fourteen-year-old in 1967 might have imagined that everyone in the gym was registering the circumference of her thighs in silent judgment, the fourteen-year-old in 2020 *knows* that they are—and there's a time-stamped screenshot of a picture from Snapchat to show it. One's self-conception becomes inextricably bound not only to the perceived feedback of others in the room but also to the documented likes and comments of those who weren't even there.

Faced with this watchful audience, kids learn to perfect their image early on. Starting in middle school, they're encouraged to think about their personal brand, to begin "engaging on the platform of your choice," to decide on their "key content areas," and ultimately to be, as Google's curriculum for "digital citizenship" puts it, "Internet Awesome." Teenagers absorb all of this at the very moment they are figuring out who that self is. It's not just that social development happens *on* social media; social media *is* social development for teenagers. It's where they learn how to be in the world and it's not technically even *in* the world. To perform their lives as much as they live their lives seems to most kids perfectly normal.

Of course, all of us perform, or act, in life according to the demands of a given situation, but in the real world, we can tailor to that situation, knowing that each sequence is for a particular audience and a particular moment. In the offline world, you wouldn't speak to the boss at work in the same way you would with a toddler at home. The early Internet likewise allowed for the possibility of shifting presentations, a place where, in text-only chats, you could explore various guises and versions of yourself.

That was early days. Today, with every bit of the Internet open to view and capture, people learn to present a single homogenized version lest they somehow slip up and stand out in the wrong way to the wrong person at the wrong moment. The coronavirus quarantine, in which everyone was forced to present online all the time, only exacerbated this process, our home selves melding with our work selves and our social selves, all of us put into BBC Dad's awkward shoes. On Facebook, you become the same "you" to your friends, your co-workers, your parents, and your future children. As Mark Zuckerberg puts it, "The days of having a different image for your work friends or co-workers and for the other people you know are probably coming to an end pretty quickly. . . . Having two identities for yourself is an example of a lack of integrity."

Is it a lack of integrity? Or is it flexibility—the ability to flub things and learn, to change, to take comfort in a deeply human inconstancy, something we rely on to stretch ourselves and grow? Isn't it okay not to worry all the time about how we come across? Perhaps people don't change dramatically in the long run, but in the normal course of life, we change in small ways all the time. We could mess up without altering our "personal brand" forever.

Now, when everyone could be watching, you decide not to make that slightly risqué toast lest someone record it, or choose not to hit the dance floor when you've had maybe one drink too many. You don't approach that total stranger. You don't tell that salty story at the holiday party unless you are certain all your listeners will keep it in the vault. You avoid making an ironic comment that could be taken out of context or viewed as sincere by someone who may not know you at all. You can't be too careful. You may choose not to post this material online, but someone else listening or watching might. Something far greater than a personal brand is lost when we cease to be uninhibited in our moments of joy, terror, pain, intimacy, and release.

16

THE SCHOOL LIBRARY

W ho didn't love the weekly escape to the school library, where you got to sit on a carpeted floor rather
than in a stiff desk chair, to listen to a story read aloud by a
librarian rather than to the teacher explaining the day's
math assignment, to find yourself captivated by a book you
would never have picked out yourself, whether because its
cover looked too dated or because it featured a squirrel?
The school librarian seemed to know exactly which one
would enchant the class each week. Even kids who weren't
readers welcomed the musty paper-and-glue smell of ancient Caldecott honorees and a time when the rowdy kids
might be quiet for just a minute, even if only through the
forceful shush of the librarian.

Then there were the rows and rows of picture books to
wander through, worlds in which you could be left alone
for a spell and someone else would put the books away
afterward. The kids who didn't have many books at home
had the freedom to choose any book they wanted. Sometimes you discovered something on your own; sometimes
you consulted the librarian, and she always seemed to
have the answer. For the bookish among us, it was the best
part of school.

But that fusty old school library has been updated, revi-
talized, and retooled for the twenty-first century. It's no

longer even called a library, but is known instead as the media center or the creation station or the new jack-of-all-trades multipurpose room (that is, we need more space). In this new space, troublesome bookshelves (walls, barriers) that formerly blocked the paths of open communication (computers) have been cleared out, and any remaining shelves have been emptied of old ideas and left largely empty of the nettlesome impediments that are books. The school will assure you that those books were outdated and that replacements should arrive in the future, budget permitting, though you may find yourself waiting for years. Meanwhile, the media center is open, collaborative, and airy enough for a free exchange of ideas to swish about—something closed books cannot offer. Students can enter and log on with ease.

All this is assuming the school library hasn't been eliminated altogether. In New York City, the number of schools with libraries fell from 1,500 in 2005 to 700 in 2014; the number of students or schools did not fall alongside it. In Britain, 22 percent of teachers reported in a recent survey that their library had suffered at least a 40 percent cut in funding since 2010, and 21 percent said their budget was insufficient to encourage students to read for pleasure.

Mind you, kids weren't the ones clamoring to abandon the school library. They already have their technology class and their school-issued laptop or tablet, and their very own smartphone and computer at home making the draw of the media center sketchy at best. Surveys and sales show that children—even screen-happy teenagers—prefer printed books to e-books by a wide margin. They also enjoy having access to free books. And it's not just kids. According to a 2016 Pew survey, 53 percent of millennials ages eighteen to thirty-five said they'd visited a library or a bookmobile in the previous year. A 2019 Gallup poll found Americans visited the library more than they went to the movies, with young adults, women, and low-income earners visiting libraries most frequently. These are people who want and like to read, and these are people who may not be able to otherwise afford those books.

But good luck to the kid looking for help figuring out what to read next, seeking advice along the lines of, "If you liked X, you might enjoy Y." Many schools, even in upscale and progressive districts like Montclair, New Jersey, no longer have a librarian on the premises. Fully 206 out of 218 public schools in Philadelphia have no librarian at all, and 200 have no library book collection. California has the worst ratio of students to school librarians in the nation: 7,000 to 1.

The logic on the part of school administrators, having invested heavily in computers, seems to be that kids can navigate their own way. If they are doing research, they can just google tidbits and resort to hunting for a book on the spare shelves only if it's truly necessary—and assuming it's even there, now that nearly all the reference books are gone. But, as the novelist Neil Gaiman put it, "Google can bring you back a hundred thousand answers. A librarian can bring you back the right one."

17

FLEA MARKET FINDS

The Fisher-Price farmhouse of my childhood included a wondrous front door that mooed every time it was pried open. How did it work?! This was not a thing for small children to understand. You could ease the door open as gingerly as you liked to see if you could outmaneuver the cow and still, out came the inevitable lowing, insistent as ever. The mystery of that door remained lodged in my mind long after the toy was gone.

So when my brother gave me a Fisher-Price farmhouse as a baby gift when my first child was born, it was like taking an express shuttle back to that childhood awe over the world's imponderables. The farmhouse he gave me was the same, if a bit grubbier than the one we'd had back at 12 Springhill Road, not some jacked-up modern rendition, which would surely have boasted more sophisticated sound effects. It was an original, of the era, from the era. He had searched for months, finally spotting it at a San

Francisco flea market, worn and uninhabited. The door still mooed.

His gift arrived by mail in 2005, just as flea markets were losing their domination of the used-goods market, before eBay and Amazon Marketplace cemented their utter conquest, making finding something special not that special anymore. In this new worldwide bazaar, an insta-Google turns up multiple vendors peddling the same thing at the same steep discount, eliminating any whiff of exclusivity or scarcity around any cool thing you own.

Gone is that sense of the quest. Happening upon a copy of an album that you've been looking for for years or spotting an out-of-print book in an out-of-town bookshop doesn't feel as much like a discovery when you could have just clicked your way there from home. You don't have to travel to northern Minnesota to try one of Betty's famous pies or to New York City for Zabar's or even to your corner supermarket for this week's groceries. There's no cool catalog in the mail, full of hard-to-find products that become unique gifts, things you would purchase by handwriting item numbers onto the enclosed order form, then repeating those numbers back to a customer service person on the phone. It took work to find the right thing. "There's something impoverishing about the current shopping experience," a friend explained. "Nothing you can give shows any effort."

We no longer have to sift through the racks at the consignment shop for a vintage dress that fits or roam through rows of household flotsam to find that one lovely teapot or pore through the pages of a catalog (farewell, Sears, Roebuck) to find the comfiest set of flannel pajamas. All of it—tons of it, more like—is available online. It's cheaper than ever, and the ease with which it can be obtained cheapens it further still. Since the founding of Craigslist in 1995, which currently lists eighty million new items each month, everything has become gettable. The hunting is easier, the chase swifter, the prey captured, usually, within minutes. You want a cockapoo? Here are forty-six freshly available pups in a sixty-mile radius—just pick the color, the sex, the breeder, the birth month. You, too, can order your own vintage Fisher-Price farmhouse or two or three, by year of fabrication and state of disrepair. They will most likely still moo, too.

18

HIGH SCHOOL REUNIONS

Anyone can be found on the Internet—actually, make that everyone, along with their address, their former addresses, their phone number, their voting record, a photo of their house, their extended genetic family, their résumé, their career path, their weddings, and their children's extracurricular activities, all in full color. We know when a distant acquaintance breaks up with her girlfriend and when a grade school classmate is dissatisfied with her job. Looks like you've moved, is it four times now?—and, oh, dear, that photo of your husband that used to feature in all of your posts has given way to photos of yourselves and the kids. Divorce? How are little Ethan and Lily taking it?

Those who might shudder at the notion of cracking open a close friend's diary feel no compunction browsing through the timeline of a third-hand social connection. The content doesn't necessarily have to be riveting to draw our attention. I have willingly sat through not one or two but *multiple* sessions of children playing piano and the violin on Facebook, children who are not my own, children of people I know only slightly. Had any of these parents invited me to attend their children's elementary school concert I would have stared at them in disbelief. It makes zero sense that I would choose to spend my limited free time watching other kids play musical instruments when I barely have enough time to watch my own kids play musical instruments. Yet here I am.

Even crazier: I don't care deeply about classical music. I don't play an instrument myself. I don't have strong feelings about any of the people whose kids I have watched playing instruments online. Every time I think about mocking someone else for some weird online habit, and lord knows we all have them, I force myself to acknowledge the abject insanity of my own. How is it that activities we wouldn't in a zillion years be roped into doing in real life—paging through an old acquaintance's baby album, suffering through an aunt's slideshow from Turkey—become strangely alluring online?

Now that we've viewed all these photos and videos, the urge to go to the next reunion to find out what the hell Jen or Dave has been up to all these years no longer holds the same sense of urgency. There is little to discover or pretend to discover, even as you go through the awkward tango of asking someone you haven't spoken to in twenty-five years what they're up to these days. You know perfectly well they have two teenage kids, a labradoodle, and a gracious split-level home in Ronkonkoma.

The last high school reunion I went to was my thirtieth, in the summer of 2019. I entered the bar with two friends I have kept in real-life touch with over the years. We split apart to make the rounds. Once again, I slipped into the same surreal, redundant small talk I'd engaged in five years earlier, with people who already knew about my work status and personal life, just as I knew about theirs. We all knew that we knew, but we went through the motions anyway as if trapped together in the same tired eighties rom-com. After three or four of these facsimiles of reunion behavior, I negotiated a path to the door I'd entered only twenty minutes earlier. Instead of swinging around again, I ducked back out and headed home, and that was fine. I was already all caught up.

Will future generations even bother with the IRL reunion every five years? Kids drag all their elementary school and high school friends along with them to college whether they want to or not. You can't leave your yearbook and your old high school acquaintances unattended in your mom's basement the way you used to. Your yearbook is everywhere.

19

"THEY FORGOT MY BIRTHDAY"

The Samantha Bakers of today will never have to endure the tragedy that befell Molly Ringwald's character in John Hughes's now-wildly-outdated 1984 movie *Sixteen Candles*. Today it's all but impossible not to know that it's someone's birthday. You cannot possibly forget.

It's on the Google calendar. Facebook sends a reminder the day before and offers a "belated" window the day after. The office intranet includes daily birthday updates for all staff members. You also know your friends' anniversary. And your friendship anniversary with them. And their work anniversary, which you are urged by email to congratulate them on when you next visit LinkedIn.

On my most recent birthday, well before my husband or kids had a chance to say a word, I received best wishes from my bank, my dentist, my GP, and my dermatologist. These greetings arrived unsolicited via text or email, presumably because at some point in the course of the business of life, I'd filled out a form, perhaps on one of those infernal padded tablets, requiring me to enter my DOB. Several other websites—someplace where I'd once bought socks for my ten-year-old, a place I'd browsed for sweatpants—chimed in with an HBD, most of them arriving in the early morn, auto-sent at 5 A.M. well before the texts and emails and balloon-filled Facebook posts appeared, many of them also from people I don't actually know.

And do any of us really *know* other people's birthdays? If someone put you on the spot and asked you to tick off all your nieces' and nephews' birthdays or the birthdays of the people who sit in the cubicles adjacent to you every day, you'd probably draw a blank. No one bothers to remember these dates. No one keeps a little notebook of birthdays or marks them next to each entry in their address book. And because you don't even have that little address book, you don't have to periodically update it or switch it out for a new one, copying the birthdays over again, committing them to memory. Don't worry; the Internet is there, all set with a birthday donation, and emojis to match. Now, if only there were a way to remember the birthdays of those few people not on the Internet. . . .

20

THE PHONE IN THE KITCHEN

The phone in the kitchen was the all-powerful hub, the portal between the family inside and the outside world, and the only way for a stranger to get into the house without physically walking through the front door. When that phone rang, everyone wanted to be the first to pick up and find out who was on the other line, even or perhaps especially when it wasn't for you. "Get off the phone!" your sister would scream from upstairs. "You can hang up now!" you called out to your dad. "Mom, he won't hang up in the kitchen!" "I can hear you breathing!" we all yelled at one another.

The phone in the kitchen always had one of those long, coiled wires that attached the receiver to the base, the better to cook by or pull into a nearby nook in an attempt at privacy. You could spend hours endeavoring to redirect the coils that exasperatingly curled in the wrong direction midway, furling and unfurling the plastic-coated wires like a Rubik's Cube. Small children, undeterred by warnings of sure death by electrocution, gnawed on them, drawn by what was an almost irresistible chewy texture and a very pleasant give. The semihard plastic tasted like toy packaging—yes, I remember it well.

It was a big deal when you were old enough to answer the phone yourself, and you were issued clear instructions: Always answer with a bright "Hello" and say, "May I tell her who's calling?" No calling after ten P.M. No calling on Sunday before noon. No talking on the phone longer than thirty minutes. *Never* make a long-distance call without asking permission! Later, when call-waiting and caller ID were introduced, certain parents thought the very concepts were "rude"—not to mention overpriced. What an extravagant notion to need to know who was calling when you could just pick up and find out! These were the same parents who, upon hearing the phone ring at an inopportune moment, glared at it, muttering, "Who on earth could be calling *now*?"

Now that almost nobody has a landline, the family phone no longer reveals the comings and goings between the people inside and outside the home. What was once transparent is opaque. Parents no longer take calls for their kids or see a log of numbers on an itemized monthly bill. The ways in which kids communicate with their friends are encrypted or ephemeral. Parents don't know whom their kids are talking to behind lock-screened devices, nor can they glean insight from overheard snippets of conversation, tearful exchanges, and slammed receivers. They don't know whom their daughter is dying to hear from, and who their son is dreading might call. Little did parents appreciate how much they could learn from a simple "Tell him I'm not home."

21

THE FAMILY MEAL

Family dinnertime was sacrosanct, no matter how close or estranged the family. Now that everyone was home from work and finished with homework, it was time to ask "How was your day." It was time for family announcements and discussions about the weekend. Certain topics could be raised strategically in front of everyone else for maximum effect; this was when you brought up things that you wanted everyone at the table to know. It was the time for conversations about Aunt Caroline's cancer and about what to do over spring break. It was the time to sulk in fury over a plain baked potato and wan broccoli, signaling to everyone at the table just how much you didn't want to be there. And you did not leave the table without asking to be excused—"May I?"—and it needed to be a good excuse.

Naturally, that family phone always rang in the middle of dinner. "Let it ring" was the prevailing ethos. Not only was it rude to pick up at dinnertime, unless Grandma was on her deathbed or someone needed picking up from the train station, it was rude to call in the first place. That had better be a telemarketer.

Now our phones are wired into mealtime, bringing the Internet to the table. We can "talk" to everyone, and we can talk to one another not at all. In restaurants, people don't converse with each other while waiting for their food. Once illuminated by candlelight, the faces of romantic couples now glow from lit-up screens. We take pictures of our food and selfies of us together and ask the waiter to take a photo, please, for good measure. You don't have to wonder what that ingredient is on the menu or betray your food ignorance by asking the waiter—you google. Even after we tuck into our food, we find convenient excuses to flip over the facedown phone or retrieve it from a pocket. It's only to check one thing, to verify something he said, to see if the babysitter texted, to answer the question Mom used to know the answer to but can't surface right now; it's going to drive her insane, so just one quick second, apologies.

The local diner is quieter, families sitting together in front of their respective devices, eyes cast downward rather than across the table, giggling to themselves or their online companions rather than with one another. Nobody is whining about not getting to order chocolate chip pancakes for lunch or asking when the food will arrive; that's all secondary. Instead, all are content, each in their own world like Pixar's postapocalyptic *WALL-E* vision of earthlings, stripped of musculature and humanity, reclining blobbily in automated loungers, affixed to portable screens.

Extracting a teenager from her phone at any meal can be such an epic struggle, it's no wonder many parents have stopped trying. Only one in three American teenagers regularly silences, turns off, or puts away her phone when visiting extended family. Of course, their parents may no longer care or even notice, because they are too busy photo-documenting the three-course meal to demonstrate their home-chef cred on Instagram. We are keto! We've gone vegetarian! We are salt of the earth and eat pork loin, but heirloom. According to one survey, only 28 percent of Americans ban phones from the dinner table.

In an experiment conducted by the University of Virginia, three hundred diners were selected at random in a café. Half were asked to keep their phones on the table and the other half to put phones away. Participants were told the experiment was about dining experiences with friends. (Phones weren't even mentioned.) After the meal, people were asked to rate their experience in terms of overall enjoyment, conversation, and the food itself. Those whose phones had been put away gave all three metrics higher ratings than those who kept their phones out during the meal, by a statistically significant factor. The meal just isn't as good. *Bon appétit.*

22

PRIVATE HUMILIATION

Before everyone carried around a camera, you could walk straight into a street pole and know that only three people saw, and two of them probably forgot it by the time they passed by, even as you stumbled and readjusted your glasses and tried to somehow make it look like you did it on purpose. During a lecture, you could blurt out a question that you might quickly realize is incredibly ignorant and possibly offensive and then sit back down and try to blend in to the dark auditorium. Or you could discover you'd been walking around the office with two squares of toilet paper affixed to the bottom of your left shoe and remove them without comment. Your minor humiliations and misfires were witnessed by a small number of people in the moment and in the immediate vicinity. You may have shared the story later with your roommate, cringing in embarrassment, and possibly been able to laugh over it, and then you'd pack it away into your mind's dark storage unit.

No longer. Perhaps knowing that someone else might document it online, when something on the embarrassing side of funny happens, you find yourself preemptively fighting the urge to make it public. You post "Look what I've spilled on my shirt!" in an effort to own it or to deflect, to in some way make it yours and then shrug it off. The shirt, at least, looks kind of nice on Instagram. The worse things look—within a certain safe zone—the more likely the compulsion to fling it out there. Now that we all can share, we do, amplifying a minor flub well beyond its natural proportions. It's almost creepy how much we've taken the call to share our lives to heart. "We'll share everything, even our worst!" we seem to be collectively assuring Mark Zuckerberg. Perhaps, if we're honest with ourselves, we do it to ward off the possibility of something truly awful happening to us and being exposed online. These are the small, superstitious sacrifices we are willing to make.

We are also willing participants in the outing of others' petty crimes, compelled to say, "I saw that." I was a witness. And I'm going to tell you about it. Whether confessing to something ourselves or calling out another person, we are ready to haul out any example from the full spectrum of little stupidities, inadvertent faux pas, and greater transgressions for group consumption, like a pulsing nation of Red Guards.

In this online update of *The Lives of Others,* you've got to watch your back because it's far easier to get caught doing anything—cheating, lying, hypocrisy, political activism on the wrong side of the political spectrum—when the Internet's enlisted soldiers are ready to tell on you. Most of us, at one point or another, find ourselves part of this fevered brigade. We all carry bugging devices and easily hidden cameras. We all have access to a mass audience. We get swept up in the emotion of taking someone down. Sometimes, the outrage we display in front of the Internet may be justified; other times, it is not. Sometimes the offender is a public figure accountable to a mass audience; other times, she who has misspoken or misstepped is a private citizen, unaccustomed to the rage of the crowd and ill-equipped to weather the force of its brutality.

And sometimes, the slipup really is a minor thing, a silly thing, the kind of foolishness that would make anyone blush hard for five minutes and then pass, unnoticed, in the unmediated world. Now it becomes a meme. What we can't do anymore, at least we don't seem able to, is keep anything to ourselves and let the moment pass undocumented. It seems only fair to let everyone in, because otherwise everything you do risks being the tree that falls in the forest. Every stupid thing. Every careless thing. You've got to own it and—as many an Internet mogul has urged us to do—share.

THE BOOKISH BOY

W hat ever happened to that kid at recess who never ventured onto the concrete or grass, but instead found a bench or a corner where he could lean against the side of the school building, unobserved, paperback in hand? He was off the radar of most other kids; maybe a few girls noticed him and developed a secret crush because he was unlike the jocks and the burnouts and the theater kids and the clowns. He was the boy who loved to read, and maybe, in the schoolyard where you grew up, he was you.

He's especially rare now. In recent years, educators, reading specialists, academics, and publishers have raised alarms about the decline in boys' reading, with the omnipresent term "reluctant reader" essentially code for "boy." The statistics they're worried about are striking: Boys are less likely than girls to cite reading as a preferred leisure activity and are far less likely to read for pleasure. According to a 2019 survey of over two thousand U.S. children, ages six to seventeen, only 49 percent of boys (versus 67 percent of girls) said they love reading; only 26 percent of boys (versus 37 percent of girls) said they read books for fun at least five days a week. Overall, the percentage of twelfth graders who read a book or a magazine every day has gone down from 60 percent in the late 1970s to 16 percent by 2016.

Guess what those boys are doing instead.

And who can blame them? The Internet, which was almost entirely designed by men, is also practically tailor-made for boys, with its endless stream of facts, statistics, sports footage, science and technology, sexual imagery, jokes, hobbies, and comics, tapping into nearly all the interests, ideas, and impulses once sought out in books. Even the most cerebral boys gravitate more toward mastering computer languages than they do toward English literature. They're playing elaborate online multiuser games with kids across town and with kids from summer camp and with kids (or maybe grown-ups?) in Belarus. They're plotting start-ups. The aspiring writers among them dream of plotting story lines not for a future novel but for a gaming company; perhaps they might one day write the code that heads off the singularity or cures cancer.

The Internet is more fun—faster, easier, and much, much bigger—than practically everything else. It sucks up the free time that's already in short supply, though when you look at the hours devoted to Internet play, it's hard to know where it all comes from. Parents of teenage boys estimate their sons spend around twenty-four hours a week playing videogames and around nineteen hours weekly on social media. That's probably just the time they know about. More than two billion people around the world are gamers, including almost half of America's population, and when they're not playing, they're watching other people play the same way people watch sports (and of course, there are e-sports). Six in ten American gamers admit to having neglected sleep, four in ten have skipped a meal, and one in five have skipped showering in order to keep playing.

Books, whatever their powers of enchantment, are not especially addictive. The vast majority of kids don't read compulsively, and certainly not when they're in the middle of a game and already feeling sleep-deprived, not when their phone is vibrating on the pillow, not when there's so much else happening in that small rectangular portal to everything else. During the entire summer of 2018, one in five kids didn't read a book—not a single one, even if the school required it. That tally was up from 15 percent only two years earlier. It's far worse for boys, with three-quarters of girls reading over the summer versus only half of boys. This persists into adulthood, with one in three grown men saying they haven't read a single book in the last year. We're running out of bookish boys to grow into bookish men (and they are missed).

WINDOW SHOPPING

Goodbye, local stationery store, pharmacy, hardware store, dress boutique, record store, haberdashery, and toy emporium. Goodbye to the seasonal storefront displays that even when dusty and neglected were still charming and occasionally outright enchanting. Goodbye, quirky shopkeepers who greet you by name or scowl at your dog and always suspect teenagers of shoplifting. Goodbye to returns and repairs, to expert advice and institutional knowledge. Goodbye to apprenticeships, to employees who were like part of the family, to recognizable faces and community gossip. To peering into a dimmed window to make out what's inside; to brightly decorated windows luring us into shops we never expected to enter; to bells on the door signaling our entry. Goodbye to grabbing your wallet and running out the door to any of these stores when you need something because it is so, so much easier just to click.

Far more often, the windows we look into are the window squares on Instagram, with their eerily targeted advertisements that know we're in the mood for fuzzy Nordic socks, or the world's most comfortable sweatpants, a bestseller just back in stock, or the dog bed that everyone is allegedly raving about. They eliminate the unfocused contemplation of window shopping, the wonder and the longing and the captivating glimpses of the unexpected.

SOLITUDE

Remember the feeling of holing up in a hotel room in a city where you knew nobody, and nobody knew where you were, and nobody was trying to get ahold of you? You were free! You didn't even have to travel to find that unleashed feeling of "I'm here, and they're over there"—you could just take a break from the hubbub by running errands all day alone, or you could wake up two hours earlier than usual and go for a long walk. These moments were yours and yours alone. Feels like a long time ago, doesn't it?

Solitude has long been considered a precious thing. As any psychologist will explain, when you know how to be by yourself and appreciate your own company, you feel better in your own skin and you function better with others. Perhaps because human beings are such relentlessly social creatures, a little solitude protects us against loneliness. This isn't just about physical isolation. True solitude is about being with your own thoughts and shutting out everyone else—with all their feelings and thoughts and needs and reactions—which has become quite difficult to do. We've gotten so good at being virtually with other people, at pinging them while we're taking that long walk or at hearting their long walk when they're on theirs, that it's made us less good at being alone. We don't necessarily appreciate whatever variation we can find on Walden any-more, which may be for the best since anything approach-ing Walden is harder than ever to find.

New technologies have always made experts worry over our sense of solitude and our ability to deal with it. Trains, for example, brought people together so easily that experts worried people would be less capable of tolerating living far apart. Radio was also considered alienating; in 1942, one report noted that Americans had become so depen-dent on radio, they could no longer deal with either soli-tude or loneliness. The more our devices aim to bring us together, the more people worry they are tearing us apart.

It's nice being able to connect at any moment. The In-ternet's permanent display of connection can be incredibly comforting—it's a wonder how we got along without it. But choosing not to share or partake can make you feel disconnected and even lonely in a situation in which you would never have felt lonely before. When no one is liking you, it feels like no one likes you. Being disconnected can feel less like delicious solitude and more like isolation.

26

PRODUCTIVITY

What the hell are we doing all day? What the hell am I? If forced to reckon with that question, I find that a typical account of my busy, busy day means ignoring many emails and answering some, likely selected from the sixty-eight messages I've starred in my in-box so as to warn myself that I absolutely must reply, ASAP. I am usually already two weeks late. I am "circling back" to the person I "touched base" with last month and only now realized never replied. I am firing off requests and follow-ups. I am circling back again, and yet again, my head whirling along, accidentally answering the same query twice, which requires a follow-up "Oops!" I zoom in and hang out within the boxy confines of Google, square-eyed with Zoom fatigue by the end of the day.

Mostly I am on Slack, which is lighting up like a twenty-first-century operator's switchboard; as soon as I extinguish one green dot, another appears, an endless game of Whac-A-Mole. All this slacking makes me feel, alas, like a slacker. But I can't stop because I've got six conversations going and I am searching for the right emoji for this thread before scrolling up the next. The unreads, the unreads, the unreads. On average, employees at large companies with one of these interoffice messaging systems send more than two hundred messages per week, according to one productivity-analytics company.

All this leads to a follow-up question: What are we accomplishing? Answer: Not much. Intended to replace onerous email accumulation, Slack and other "team-collaborative applications" often only compound the problem. Now we've got notifications across multiple channels and we're wondering what's going on in the channels that we're not in but perhaps should be. (Must check on that later.) Chat in its various formats has gone from being a minuscule part of the workday to the second most common computer activity after email.

We do a lot of checking. We check our laptops, our desktops, and our occasionally godforsaken voicemail when one shows up, even if only to delete the cryptic-to-the-point-of-insane transcription of spam messages left in Mandarin. In one recent survey, 50 percent of employers said cellphones were distracting their employees; 44 percent of employers said the Internet in general was a distraction. In another, 73 percent of people said technology had become too distracting altogether. What was it distracting us from?

27

LETTERS TO THE EDITOR

Letters to the editor were the way that regular people, people who didn't necessarily have power in the wider world, let the people who *did* have power know what they were thinking. It was one of the few avenues for readers and citizens to be heard by politicians and business leaders and public figures, and by the journalists who wrote about them. It was a rare way to see your name in print and pretty much the only way for most people to get their perspective in front of a mass audience. In a letter to the editor, you could, for instance, complain that there were no crossing guards working a major intersection or that an article that ran last week contained misleading information about the local utility. You could raise awareness.

Most letters to the editors weren't rants or taunts or explosions of spleen. They were considered and they were *edited*. Dedicated letters editors sorted through them, weeding out any that seemed dishonest or unhinged or factually unsound. What eventually got published were critiques and suggestions and, very occasionally, compliments. They included deliberated responses from organizations, ad hoc groups, and individual readers, and they were signed and dated, holding the letter writers accountable for their own words; they even occasionally made an impact.

Because it was such a big deal to have your particular letter selected for print, people generally took care with what they wrote. You had to type up your missive, find an envelope, and track down where the heck the stamps were. You had to carry your letter to the nearest mailbox and wait several days to see if your carefully crafted thoughts might appear. All this work meant you had to feel pretty darn strong about the issue to bother.

Not surprisingly, most people, in the end, wouldn't write the letter. Maybe they'd contemplate it in the heat of the moment, even compose a few lines; then a few hours might go by, after which the movie critic didn't seem sexist anymore or the article that important. Perhaps there were other things to do than spend time writing a letter about whatever it was that got you worked up in the first place.

Now, of course, the moment that white flash of pique strikes, you just fire off an email to the editor. The object of your indignation needn't know it's you because you can use a fake or anonymized account. You can curse away. Tell the writer she's ugly, stupid, incompetent, not qualified, and should let some younger or better person have the job she is selfishly clinging to. And why take the trouble of writing to the editor at all when you can get at the true source of your ire, whether it's a politician, actor, director, or local bureaucrat, in so many other ways? Any number of direct lines are faster and easier than email and more immediately rewarding; you can post a four-part tirade on Twitter or go on NextDoor and @ the town comptroller or unleash in the comments of a related article or

Facebook post. Nobody, not an editor nor any other gate-keeper, can stop you. This is certainly more democratic, should the object of your complaints see what you're saying. But now that everyone can speak out in a public forum, it may be harder than ever to get heard amid the onslaught. We are all shouting at once.

28

LOSING YOURSELF IN A SHOW

As soon as the theater lights dimmed, the outside world faded away, and it stayed away for two hours. This was a joy if the show was, say, *Anna Christie* or *Hedwig and the Angry Inch,* and closer to torture if you were stuck center row at *Starlight Express,* but whether you loved or hated it, joining an audience meant there was nothing to do but let go of whatever might be happening outside the theater and lose yourself in what was happening onstage. It's not like there was any choice. You simply couldn't be reached. If the babysitter was unable to put the baby down or your ex-boyfriend was drunkenly banging on your front door or you had a letter from your grandmother waiting in your mailbox, it would have to continue waiting for the curtain to come down and for you to get home. You were *at a show.*

The worst interruption might be the loud crinkle of a sourball candy wrapper or the kid farthest away from the aisle needing to pee halfway through Act One. Someone might spontaneously sing along or loudly ask their neighbor what just happened. At the school concert, things were a bit looser; there was a good chance of an overzealous parent or two leaning into your sight path in order to get a decent view of their own kid. The person next to you at the stadium concert might flick repeatedly at a broken lighter during the encore ballad.

None of this compares to the circus atmosphere of even the most serious theater audience today. Despite the announcements—the outright pleas—at the start of any show to get us to please silence our cellphones, to not record, to not use flash photography, and to kindly respect the performers, nobody seems to turn their phones off at the theater. Oh, they silence them, sure, but they don't shut them down entirely because—and you know this yourself—it would take too long to power back up later, and people simply cannot stand to disconnect. So even as you sit there trying to immerse yourself in the performance, you can still hear the low buzz from your jacket pocket, as can your neighbors, tugging attention ever so slightly from the drama onstage. (Did your boss just reply to that memo?) We can also see that person three rows ahead plunging an arm into her bag to check her phone from within, screen dimmed in a half-hearted attempt at discretion. It's no use, madam. We see you.

Most pop music concerts allow for upheld phones, no matter how disconcerting to the performer. But what's new is the sheer ubiquity of those intent on capturing the entire show for posterity. "Could you stop filming me with that video camera? Because I'm really here in real life," the singer Adele said to a fan during a European concert tour. "This is a real show."

29

THE ROLODEX

Heavyset and imposing, the Rolodex stood guard next to the multiline phone on the desks of the top brass; sometimes several were lined up in a demonstration of might, a nerve-racking sight to behold during a job interview. "This guy knows everyone," you'd think to yourself, along with the corollary, "I'm no one." As soon as you got your first desk job, you would order a black Rolodex of your own from the office supply catalog, a baby step on your way up. You tried to fill it in with any business card you could get, your friends' cards, your mom's even, just so it wouldn't look bare. A Rolodex had to be well stuffed to make clear that you knew people—lots of people, important people, unlisted people—and that you knew how to get in touch with them.

"You are who you know," the expression went, and it meant that you were what we then called "connected." From the moment it was invented in 1956 for the *Mad Men* era, the spiral-bound, rotating card-containing device whose name was a portmanteau of the words "rolling index" was the follower count of its day, separating the riff-raff from the muckety-mucks. And unlike today's friend lists, it was impenetrable to outsiders.

Those heavy plastic monoliths have since nearly vanished, along with the Don Drapers who flicked through them with ruthless authority. The brand itself has been repurposed for the digital era as a form of "contact management," an organizational meld you're supposed to complete with your various online address books, which indeed feels like a Sisyphean task worthy of professional assistance. "Who *are* all these people?" you may find yourself wondering as you peruse your own contact list. We are all Kevin Bacon–level connected, but few of us actually know our connections.

30

RELYING ON THE DOCTOR

Remember what it was like having a mysterious bump on your arm and no clue what it could be? Either it was a mosquito bite or it was skin cancer. It could be a mole you'd somehow never noticed before, or a mole that had morphed into something less benign overnight. Oh my god, it could be Lyme. You just didn't know and how could you possibly? Trying to describe a random bump to a friend—even to a doctor friend—over the phone (before phones had cameras) was impossible. You made an appointment and waited it out because there was no other option.

You would have to wait not only hours but more likely days before you could get into a doctor's office for a consultation. You could spend those days contemplating the bump, but you'd have no way to situate yourself on the spectrum between calm reassurance and darkest imaginings. Once you saw your doctor, you'd be so eager for a diagnosis that whatever she said you would cling to as the word of God. Finally, an answer. Unless it was serious enough to warrant seeking a second opinion, you took her conclusions as definitive.

What you couldn't do was conduct an extensive image search of the rash beforehand, freak out over three potential rare genetic disorders, dive down a medical rabbit hole with Dr. Google, and emerge a seasoned expert, albeit one who is mortally ill. You wouldn't have considered a full constellation of associated symptoms and landed on a probable self-diagnosis. (It was either Kawasaki syndrome or fibromyalgia or West Nile!) You wouldn't come to that initial appointment armed with theories, ready to challenge the doctor on her diagnosis or insist she read a study you printed out from MedlinePlus.

But now that you have all that information, the photos, the data, the possible avenues of treatment, the shared personal stories, you will have thoughts to impart by the time your appointment rolls around. You will have been through a full journey of fact-finding and a world of emotion by the time you walk into that doctor's office. Of course, you didn't wait for the doctor to start taking oregano oil for your Lyme, and you may think you know something about that rash that she doesn't. She will want to throttle you as you tell her all about it.

31

BEING FIRST

Oh, for the days when you could be the first person to walk by a sample sale or discover an art gallery or find a great boutique hotel off the beaten track in Prague. You could be the first to access exclusive information: to get wind that the algebra teacher was pregnant well before it was public knowledge, or see that cool indie band with your older brother before anyone else knew they even existed. For a moment you were the only one you knew who knew. You got to ride that wave for a moment longer still before telling your friends and loved ones. It was so satisfying to be the source.

Now someone else always gets to the hidden swimming hole before you do. Sometimes that person gets to the virtual swimming hole first only to respond with a ludicrous "first!" that signals neither taste nor knowledge nor accomplishment, but merely a kind of doggedness, a lying-in-wait quality that means, quite possibly, nothing other than the willingness to hit the refresh button and a lot of free time. For some, getting there first is all there is, but you don't even know what that feels like because you are never that person. Whoever that person is, she claimed all the good stuff on Amazon Vine. She already knew about that pop-up store you just drove by and has been posting about it on her Substack for days. She surfaced that feed hours ago, found the Easter egg, started the thread, and created the gif that became a meme. Before you knew about any of this, her post went viral and she's well on her way to becoming an influencer.

Online, it is obvious and quantifiable how far ahead everyone else is. Your clever take has been taken. You may think your taste is esoteric and that your tea towel collection has a quirky-chic aesthetic all its own, but you can bet that someone else has already posted a significantly better collection on Pinterest. Turns out, lots of people collect your special thing—whatever it is—and have showcased their well-lit treasures already. Several established fan clubs boast a number of devoted followers you'll never catch up to. You're just another fanboy in a long line, one whose dedication may look pretty lame compared with that of the true devotees and diehards. You are, in fact, last.

Even those among us who never pretended to be pioneers might nonetheless be deflated by the clear and ever-present evidence that we're perennially late to the party. That our outfit is nothing new and has been worn better. That the out-of-print novel from the 1930s you discovered has been subjected to a full night's sky of stars on Goodreads. The "new" hole-in-the-wall Lebanese takeout in your hood has been rated on Yelp and Eater and Chowhound and is sprouting a branch in Greenpoint. You didn't start anything; you only just caught on.

32

BEING THE ONLY ONE

A t one point or another in life, and for some of us more than once, each of us has been seized by the paranoid conviction that we were the only one to think X or be Y or do Z. It was that feeling that you were the alien and everyone else was of this earth, or else maybe . . . *they* were the aliens and you, alas, the sole earthling. You were caught in *The Matrix, The Truman Show,* a seventies conspiracy movie, the only sane person left on the planet, or perhaps the only one not in on the joke. It was an awful and oppressive feeling.

There is zero chance of feeling that way now. Online, you can always find the one other person just like you, or the two or three or four thousand. There's tremendous comfort in knowing that while you may not be that special or remarkable, you are also not alone or (that) weird. If you're the parent of a child with high-needs autism or if you lack mobility or have a rare medical condition; if you live in an isolated community or feel isolated from the people in your community—the Internet is a godsend. It is no longer next to impossible to find someone dealing with the exact same issue or circumstance, whether you're a gender-fluid teenager or a young widow. People who would otherwise be strangers are out there and they are there for you—on forums and in chat rooms and via a myriad of specialized websites. You can always consult and commiserate with your people.

The Internet world is easier on the shy folk and the wallflowers, a place where people are far more approach-able than in real life. It's less risky to DM someone or tag them than it is to walk up to them in a crowded room or a silent hallway and ask them out. The stakes seem much lower. For people who have social anxiety, online communication can be a lifeline. Even for the somewhat less anxious, online connection is simpler, easier, and faster than the clunky offline mode. The stakes of online friendship are lower—you never have to go out of your way for someone you know exclusively on Instagram beyond tapping a button—and yet being tapped by someone else can feel like affirmation.

A kid doesn't have to leave the house to find someone to hang out with or ask her mother for permission to take the bus to the mall. The myriad apps where kids can con-gregate, lurk, befriend, and unfriend takes them well be-yond the confines of the school cafeteria, where they may barely talk to one another at all, wolfing down lunch while catching up with other kids on their phones. Those who can't find their people at school can find them somewhere else. Sixty percent of teenagers spend time with their friends online on a daily or near-daily basis, and at night they often go to sleep with their best friend, worst fren-emy, and longtime crush lying right next to them, digitally.

33

BIRTHDAY CARDS

Kids' birthdays began with a dash to the mailbox, waiting for that first trickle of oversized envelopes, which often arrived days ahead of time because what doting aunt would want her birthday wishes to miss the big day? That youthful excitement endured well into adulthood even when the cards, purchased in museums and stationery stores, no longer contained pop-ups and foldouts, checks or stickers, but instead a more adult version of birthday deliciousness—caring notes about friendship and family.

Now, birthday greetings may instead arrive in the form of emails, posts, texts, and, perhaps worst of all, e-cards, which either slip into spam where they belong or land in unison on the morning of the big day because they are automated. However they get there, nobody wants them. Really, nobody. Ready-made and free for anyone who signs up and signs away their data (and yours!), the e-card says nobody could be bothered making or buying a card of their own. There is nothing fun about the e-card, which forces you to click through several slow-to-load screens before you arrive at anything resembling a personal message. It leaves no recipient feeling seen or tended to. It feels crappy on your birthday, indifferent on Valentine's Day, brutal on Mother's Day.

There may not even be an e-card if a birthday gift arrives in multiple shipments via Amazon with its sole message a generic "Happy Birthday! Love, Grandma" printed in ten-point sans serif type on the packing slip alongside sterile return instructions, or if your present is an online gift card with only a line filled out with the name of giver and recipient. At least you don't have to write a real thank-you note either.

34

A GOOD NIGHT'S SLEEP

Squeeze shut those bleary eyes and think back to what it was like when you could turn out the lights knowing that everyone else—at least within your time zone—had also called it a night. There was no party-after-you-left situation—it was just good night, people. The world stopped its incessant chatter and shut down. Only when the morning paper arrived and the commute began were we all brought back onto the same page. Think what it was like to be a teenager when you could rest assured that at a certain point every day, you no longer had to fear that your friends were gathering without you or whispering behind your back. Of course they weren't. They were asleep.

But who can sleep when the Internet is there? There's no such thing as sleep when you're waiting for an overdue email that hasn't materialized, or when someone posted an inexplicable and upsetting comment on that photo you shared right before bedtime. Why? Just, why? You will ponder it pillowside for hours, pausing from your worry to check the phone yet again for a possible explanation. It (you) cannot wait until morning.

Study after study shows that using devices at bedtime results in poor sleep, which isn't good news for the 70 percent of adult Americans who sleep with a phone by their side. The disturbing alternative is to give up the Internet for eight (let's dream a little) straight hours—but how can you do that when there's one last email you realize you need to send just as you're drifting off at eleven, and then while there, why not check and see if anyone posted anything crucial? If you bolt awake at four A.M., you can work in a surreptitious peek and wind up doomscrolling into the morning, appalled at both the world and yourself. Have you ever found yourself using that four A.M. wake-up to "get ahead" on the morning's email? I have.

It's not our fault. "Your cortisol levels are elevated when your phone is in sight or nearby, or when you hear it or even think you hear it," says David Greenfield, professor of clinical psychiatry at the University of Connecticut School of Medicine and founder of The Center for Internet and Technology Addiction. "It's a stress response, and it feels unpleasant, and the body's natural response is to want to check the phone to make the stress go away." When you're switched on all the time, the ability to push the off button becomes not only inconvenient, but impossible. Psychologists call this "continuous partial attention." It's not relaxing.

If, for some reason, the Internet doesn't keep us up at night, it will zing us out of bed in the morning. Here I am, it says with a vibrating workout reminder, or an intoning chime reminding us to meditate as it delivers the latest grim updates from around the world and tallies our unreads with fearsome notifications. Eight in ten smartphone users check their phones within fifteen minutes of waking and by golly, we must. If—heaven forbid—we actually slept through the night, we need to know what we missed.

KNOWING THE NUMBER

My best friend's phone number was 944-6327. Mine was 944-7091. When we were growing up, everyone could reel phone numbers off at will: Your mom at work. The pediatrician. The school. The preferred pizza delivery.

Now, of course, we know nobody's number, and I mean nobody's. I barely recognize my own, nor do I know the phone numbers of my own children, nor can I fully believe that two of them even have their own phone numbers. Having your own phone line used to be a huge deal! (And our grandparents walked three miles just to get to school . . .)

A short time ago, while visiting Cambridge, I made a plan for coffee with a friend I hadn't been in touch with for twelve years. He suggested we exchange mobile information so we could text each other our respective whereabouts. "Are you still 917-XXX-XXXX?" he wrote. I stared at the number in question. It was familiar, though not persuasively so. After a few moments of fixed concentration, I concluded that while the number may have been mine at one time, I couldn't say for certain. I remembered my number from childhood but could not recognize my number from only a decade earlier.

THE PAPER

Mornings were for the paper, to be read over coffee, exchanging sections with a roommate or enjoying it on your own so you could tear out whatever you pleased. Morning commutes were for the paper, folded up on the subway so you could turn the pages in a tight space like an expert. Brunch was for the paper, pleasingly enormous on Sundays, splayed out over a too-small restaurant table, after a long wait to be seated. Of course, I feel these losses keenly because I work at a newspaper—but I felt this way long before I worked there. Reading "the paper" was something all grown-ups did, and as an aspiring grown-up from an early age, it was something I wanted to do, too.

Everyone had his section back when newspapers had sections. The sports fan turned immediately to the sports pages. From baseball to basketball, the paper was where you checked schedules, statistics, trades. If you fell asleep before the game ended, you'd have to wait to find out what happened in the morning paper, or, occasionally, the eve-

ning news on TV. Early papers on the East Coast often
didn't get the West Coast scores in time for deadline.

If you were in a fantasy baseball league, you'd pore over
the statistics, making long calculations, then xerox the results and send them around to the rest of your league.
Every week on Tuesdays and Wednesdays, *USA Today*
would print figures for every state, and one person in the
league would take on that task. "This was in the nineties,"
a friend of mine recalled. "When I think of it now it feels
like we lived in the 1800s." In the 2020s, a website calcu-
lates all that for you. When it comes to news, getting information in a way that cannot be refreshed every minute
feels like ambling over to the village square and waiting for
the town crier to show up.

Vital information was once available only in the paper,
often in formats that required time and skill to interpret.
Learning to read the box scores in baseball was a rite of
passage, with a dad or older brother taking you through
the steps. If you wanted to know stock prices, you had to
learn how to sift through and interpret the tables in the
business section. Before real-time online trading, most financial amateurs (that is, people who didn't work in fi-
nance) relied on some combination of those inscrutable
tables and a broker (who had to be paid) to carry out any
transaction. The average joe couldn't place a trade without
a gatekeeper—one with the expertise and experience to
prevent you from making a fast and foolish decision.

Depending on your local paper wasn't just about keeping up on the news or indulging your passion, whether it
was sports or the comics. You needed the coupons and you
needed the classifieds, which were your gateway to financial independence and that first hole-in-the-wall apartment

downtown. Until you got there, your mom would clip articles of interest and send them to you by mail, neatly folded into a business envelope—the review of a new movie you might like, stories about cities you'd visited together, an article about the neighbor's exemplary son.

The local paper celebrated your daughter's soccer game victory. It noted the names of this year's graduates and the ones who made the dean's list. It's where you published an engagement announcement that you could clip and save, embossing or framing it for posterity; a printout from the digital version does not look the same. You knew that your great-aunt, a fixture in her little southern Illinois town for eight decades, would get an obituary describing the hours she gave to her church and her neighbors and friends. You could trace the trajectory of an entire life in the pages of the paper, from birth announcement to sports victories to death, in ink and paper—the stuff of life that is now recorded in bright digital imagery on Facebook, seen by your friends and your "friends," but not by your local community.

37

UNPOPULAR OPINIONS

These are not the careless and carefree days when one foolish remark made on a Tuesday afternoon in front of a few people will be forgotten by Thursday. Today, when every expressed thought is voted up or down, liked or ignored, and texted to someone else so it can be made fun of and potentially used against you, you learn to watch what you say. And unless you're a troll or an irrepressible contrarian or a masochist, you learn not to say anything that could be taken the wrong way, especially if your opinion is political in nature or has any bearing on anything consequential, controversial, or remotely important in the world taking place outside your window.

Before everyone toted an Internet megaphone, most people didn't bother telegraphing their every passing pensée and opinion for public dissection, mostly because the baseline assumption was that nobody really cared what you thought; people kept their own counsel. Once we were all given a platform to stand on, the ground-level assumption was that we all had something to say and should speak up. Who knew how much we were holding in all that time?

Well, now we know, so we know how it goes. Sure, we can—and should—speak up, but only with the utmost care and only when we know everyone who hears is on the same side you're on. Voiced opinions must fit into one of several predetermined buckets placed at safe distance in a deeply polarized social, political, and cultural landscape. Once you are accounted for and have fallen safely in line, those sharing your bucket will pat you on the back for your right-think. You are either an ally or you are the enemy. In this world of enforced popular opinion, few will dare risk saying something that falls into the muddy middle, something that may lead to a vitriolic pile-on from all corners, both known and distressingly anonymous. It looks like we're speaking up and speaking out, but most opinions are relentlessly held in check by the crowd; we all play it safe.

Those safe opinions may not be interesting ones or enlightening ones or informative ones, or even informed ones. Those safe opinions will not be provocative, at least not to their established group of tuned-in listeners who are already in preset agreement. Those opinions may not even truly be your own. We hear what we want to hear and say what we think we should say, brushing aside the sorry fact that these opinions with all the edges burnished off do not necessarily trump the opinion of a single person who dares have a challenging or unpopular thought.

But it's the smart road to take because the Internet is always listening. It magnifies the tiny moment and amplifies the petty and the ephemeral into something that feels enormous and eternal.

And the Internet comes for us all one day.

It comes armed with denouncements and pushback and cyberbullying's most brutal punishment: cancellation. Even before that reckoning, you can be called out or ratioed; you can cycle through a month's worth of turbulent emotions within a matter of seconds, reacting, overreacting, second-guessing yourself and decrying the world, brooding and just beginning to settle down, only to find something else provocative to rile you right back up. In the worst thralls of it, it becomes hard to catch your breath, hard to gain perspective, hard not to feel like the world is dead set against you. We've lost the natural pace of regaining any sense of equilibrium.

38

SOLO TRAVEL

When traveling by yourself meant traveling alone, you'd fill up a backpack, buy a Eurail pass, maybe procure a courier ticket—half price because you had to drop off a mysterious packet in Hong Kong—and then wave goodbye at a big send-off with family or friends, knowing you wouldn't see them for two weeks or two months. You were on your own.

Traveling by yourself meant neither seeing nor communicating with the world back home for the full duration of the trip. It meant there was no way to ask a trusted acquaintance for a restaurant recommendation or to tell your friends back home about the insane youth hostel manager or the loud snorer on the overnight train. You couldn't consult your entire friend group on a decision about whether to take the overnight bus or splurge for the train or to skip Hoi An in favor of Nha Trang. That was on you. No one could marvel in real time at what you were seeing and on what budget; you had to rely on your own reactions and personal opinions. You had to jot them down to remember them and to keep your own company.

When the not-talking and not-sharing started to get to you, you would seek out companionship wherever you could get it, even if it meant exchanging backpacker tips in broken English with that goofy German guy in the Guns

N' Roses T-shirt, or carrying on long conversations with the Italian waiter in something more closely resembling Spanish on your end—just to hear the sound of your own voice somewhere other than in your head.

Nobody knew where you were—they couldn't locate you, track you, or contact you. You were untethered. You were free. Out there unobserved, you let go of the way in which you might be perceived. You didn't do something just because you might be expected to or so you could post about it. You'd stop at a scenic view and stay longer than anyone else might tolerate or skip it altogether because you didn't want to plan your staring according to designated signposts. You didn't have to pretend to be transfixed by the *Mona Lisa*—you could even bypass the museum altogether, damn it.

When you traveled alone in the Before Internet, you looked around rather than down. You saw and noticed other people, and they saw you. You had encounters with strangers. The people from back home—your sister and her latest argument with Dad, your partner and his crap sales presentation, your crush who never gave you a second thought—could be put out of mind. This kind of delirious freedom is impossible now, when the outside world is always only a microsecond away, beckoning you to touch base.

39

PAPERWORK

What was this paperwork of which you speak, asks the Gen Z worker. And this "pushing papers" people once supposedly engaged in?

Let us, for their sake, recount the pleasures: There was so much paperwork, it could fill several large rectangular boxes in the span of a week, and it was so important, it had to be taken into deep storage, and it was on you to make sure no papers slid from their manila moorings, fluttering to the floor, one sheet sliding irretrievably under a cabinet. (Remember: We had those file cabinets to fill.) Those documents that weren't kept were shredded in a machine whose acoustics rivaled the leaf blower, and it would spill a good many crinkle chips of paper onto the floor, no matter how carefully you tumbled the remnants into the recycling.

There was the endless time you spent standing by the Xerox machine, watching that it didn't jam or run out of paper or collate the papers incorrectly or inadvertently print something doubled-sided (your boss hated that). Then you had to circulate all that material—the distribution lists, the handouts, the packets—all of which you placed into in-boxes across the fifth floor. There was the odious typing of addresses onto envelopes, which you'd scroll up and down the typewriter wheel, hoping they didn't get accordioned in the process, never quite figuring out how to perfectly center the information, and when you finally did, there was a typo. Wite-Out.

In the pre–Google Docs, Dropbox, PDF days, you received a thick binder before the big meeting or conference, reams of papers that you would physically go through and mark up, unlike the environmentally friendly PowerPoints that somehow never feel like required reading. These ether-only documents are circulated in open, scattered, flexible offices that are quite possibly remote and almost entirely paper-free.

Without a designated workspace, there can be no nameplate or floating globe desk toy, and you never generate enough paper to justify a paperweight. All the desktop tchotchkes are in a mad fight against obsolescence since there is often no more desk for them in the old-timey furniture sense of the word.

The deadly letter opener is gone, as is the killer staple remover. If you persist in doing things like a Pilgrim, you might find a paper clip or its hardier modern cousin, the binder clip, on a shelf in a stockroom. You don't need a standing rack to store receipts in because your receipts are digitized. The fax never rings, which is helpful since nobody knows where the fax machine is anymore or what it is. Bartleby the Scrivener has left the building, taking his attaché with him.

40

MISSED CALLS

Missing a phone call was a big deal. A phone call offered excitement and mystery and possibility. For all you knew, it could have been the call that would have changed your life. It could have been the boy you'd fantasized about since fifth grade on the line, finally recognizing your innate beauty—who, faced with your failure to pick up, loses his nerve and never calls again. Maybe it was the school principal trying to reach your parents, and you could have effectively intercepted it, promising to pass along a message. Maybe you'd won the lottery!

Sometimes you ran into the house to answer the phone only to pick up to a dial tone. (Ah, the dial tone—and jiggling the lever trying to get one.) Sometimes you stuck around the house for hours waiting for the phone to ring. Everyone else had gone to the pool, and there you were, sitting by the refrigerator because that guy said he "might" call you this weekend—for all you knew he went to the pool with them.

Lost calls, missed calls, unreturned calls. Not knowing who was calling—your grandma, someone to whom you owed money, a person who wanted to hire you or fire you, a wrong number. Calls that were just plain mistakes: The first call you made to a 900 number (daily horoscope, favored celebrity), not knowing each additional minute cost

$2.95. Times you resorted to calling the time lady because nobody remembered to wear a watch, or the clock's battery had run out. The occasional blackout, when everyone who owned only a cordless phone felt like an idiot because they had inadvertently cut themselves off from the world.

For a hefty fee of 75 cents, you could press *69 to retrieve the number of the last person who called, assuming that person was listed, and, for all you knew, it was the number of someone you didn't want to talk to. You could spend weeks playing phone tag. "I left you another message," you could say. It may have been true. Much of the time, you could just pretend. "I tried calling again but it was busy!"

Your life could depend on one missed call. Think *Dial M for Murder.* Think *Are You in the House Alone?* Think *Scream.* Fingers fumbling over the rotary, the receiver wrung from the heroine's hands. In *The Terminator,* a cyborg arrives on earth to seek out and destroy Sarah Connor's life. He comes from the future, embodying its most cutting-edge technologies, an invincible amalgam of robot and human strength. Does he use his embedded GPS system to search her down? Does he find her with his DNA-detecting sensory system? Does he perceive her presence through the movement of an array of electrons uniquely coded to her body? He does not. Instead, he relies on the most advanced technology available to humans at the time, which was 1984: He looks her up in the white pages.

The answering machine—remember that glorious innovation?—answers the Terminator with a goofy, self-conscious stream of words, trying to trick the caller into thinking Sarah Connor herself has answered. "Fooled ya!" Connor's recorded voice crows. Across town and frantic, aware she is in danger, our heroine locates a pay phone. These tense scenes held the viewer of 1984 on the edge of his seat. Today it feels like watching a lumbering horse-drawn carriage in *Little House on the Prairie*, trying to reach the lower field in time to till the potatoes.

41

THE SPANISH-ENGLISH DICTIONARY

Poor translations. Blunders and repeated misunderstandings. Not even attempting an accent because it's far too embarrassing to hear yourself or be heard trying to sound French. These were the regular failures of trying to speak a foreign language when you had nothing but a pocket dictionary or the brief appendix in your travel guide and a couple of years of indifferent high school French. *"Gai plau,"* I told the waiter in beginner Thai, the day I moved to Thailand in 1993, convinced I was ordering chicken. The waiter nodded and returned with an omelet over a heap of rice. Humbled and confused and worried about what I might get if I hazarded a correction, I ate it anyway. The following day, I went to another restaurant, tried again, got the exact same thing.

There was no Google Translate or YouTube language pro or Duolingo or "translate this page" or audio clips to check intonation. By the time I learned I was pronouncing the "g" too hard and saying *kai plau*, egg and rice, I preferred the omelet to the chicken anyway, something I never would have known had I gone online for help. You learn surprising things about a culture when you make your way through its language without high-tech assistance. You learn, as we all know, through your mistakes and through your mispronunciations.

No more. We need not veer onto a side road of trial and error. We need not commiserate over the mutual inability to understand each other or, conversely, find out that we can manage to get through with no words at all, laughing at our silly hand gestures and exaggerated facial expressions in what may look to all appearances like an impromptu game of charades. In a world where everyone speaks Internet, learning a foreign language may become as obsolete as studying Latin or memorizing the periodic table, nothing more (in some people's eyes) than an impressive party trick and an extravagant waste of time.

Google Translate does it all on your behalf. With the miraculous click of a button you can read a website written in French or Farsi. You can understand a sentence written in many languages from around the entire world within seconds. You can practice your pronunciation over and over until it's as near perfect as it's going to get for a nonnative speaker with no particular gift for foreign tongues. When I suggest to my kids that they check a Spanish-English dictionary while doing their homework, they practically laugh in my face.

[42]

PATIENCE

O nce there was a time for everything, and you had to
wait for it. That meant sitting tight until six P.M. for
the evening news to tell you what terrible things you
needed to know and then until prime time for appointment television in order to relax once you knew them. You
counted down the months for an entire year before you
could watch *The Sound of Music, The Wizard of Oz,* and *It's
the Great Pumpkin, Charlie Brown,* which arrived according
to season with the mesmerizing swirl of the CBS Special Presentation logo spinning to a drumbeat crescendo.
There was no recording and there was no rewinding, and
the calendar year always ended when Frosty the Snowman
made his annual visit. Half the joy was in the run-up of
previews that infiltrated your weekly dose of Saturday
morning Scooby Doo, the only time of the week in which
such cartoons appeared, and thus, also something you had
to wait for.

The VHS player, and, to a lesser degree, the Betamax,
revolutionized viewing habits by offering some modicum
of control for the very first time. In the eighties, teenagers
would spend hours watching bad videos on MTV in the
hopes that eventually, the video they wanted would come
on, rushing the VCR in the first few seconds—always getting it just a moment too late—so that they might record it

and have power over their viewing the next time. We did the same thing with the radio, endlessly rotating the dial in search of music that was our own, fingers on the play and record button, ready to press them down simultaneously.

Suppose you wanted to watch an Olympic feat? That took four years because you couldn't call up highlights from the last Games on YouTube when there was no YouTube. Want to see that touchdown again? In the eighties, you could rent a DVD of greatest plays from Blockbuster (and then traipse back to return it) or wait for a special to surface on ESPN. Waiting, waiting, waiting.

Even renting a video from Blockbuster had its inconveniences: pulling on shoes, pulling out of the driveway to face traffic, pulling into the video store in that little strip mall that never had enough parking and then wandering around wondering if what you were seeking would be shelved in Action or Thrillers or Newly Released and lamenting the fact that nobody ever, ever, properly alphabetized the containers. You might get there only to wait in line for twenty minutes because some lady forgot to bring her membership card, only to find that the person in front of you just took out the last available copy of the movie you wanted, so new and desirable that it was stored behind the counter.

In the early days of the Internet, things still took longer. Remember the minute-long interval in which our modems dialed up a connection, a window opened, and the AOL mailbox icon appeared announcing, "You've got mail"? Today, the opening sequence to the Nora Ephron movie of the same name looks like slo-mo. For contemporary comparison, think about the micro-interval between the plane touching down on the tarmac and the moment when your phone, which you rescue from airplane mode, offers a working signal. Why must it take *so long,* you wonder. Your battery is charged. You've got two bars. Where is your carrier? Where is the cascade of incoming messages? Why isn't your phone letting you send that text? The wait is interminable.

The once ubiquitous progression of discovery, anticipation, patience, impatience, and—wait for it . . . finally!—gratification is alien to anyone under the age of fifteen; they can't fathom the notion of a time slot. Seventy percent of video viewing by millennials is "time-shifted," meaning it is watched at a time other than its original broadcast. Nobody waits for the next episode when they can binge-watch the whole darn thing. There's no more sense of we're-all-in-this-together when even a live football game and a presidential debate can be paused for a beer run. You can always rewind a precise fifteen seconds to catch that scrap of dialogue you missed. You can watch whatever you want whenever you want it. You never have to get stranded on *Gilligan's Island* because there is always, always something else on when you want to see it.

43

IGNORING PEOPLE

It was useful to pretend to have no idea someone was trying to reach you when you could actually get away with it. How could you have known? You were out, you were sleeping, you were busy, you were away, you had an emergency, you didn't get the message and you are only just hearing about this now. It was possible and believable to be off the grid. Someone else could pick up the landline when it rang and say you weren't home. If you worked in the office, someone else could answer the phone and tell them you were unavailable. Sorry!

Being online is like constantly being asked on a playdate with the kid you've been desperately trying to avoid, the kid who always manages to know where you are, lurking around the edge of your friend group, his mom cornering your mom at pickup time. You could figure your way out of even those vexing situations. But the Internet is insistent and doesn't take no for an answer or even take a hint. The Internet is the fake-personal text from the veterinarian's office wondering how your pet is doing, or the ophthalmologist asking you to check their secure one-way communication delivery system. The Internet is the pesky email asking how you liked your meal delivery, whether you were happy with your dry cleaning, whether you're aware of your daughter's gymnastics meet. Our phones buzz and ping with endless missives from realtors, medical practices, clothing vendors, LinkedIn updates, and actual people—all of them wanting.

44

DITTOS

D ittos were an even more significant part of the educational system paper complex than fill-in-the-oval answer booklets and three-ring binders and composition books with mottled black-and-white covers. In many ways, classwork was defined by the ceaseless parade of dittos, reams and reams of photocopied worksheets. No sooner was one set completed than another got passed out, down one row and up the next.

Dittos kept you busy. Dittos filled up the day. Dittos went home and came back the next morning. Occasionally, dittos were intended to challenge students, but often seemed more like they were there to school you into submission. Most kids learned to tolerate them, but some annoyingly obedient and studious kids (okay, me) secretly loved their clear beginnings and finite ends. Teachers marked up dittos with easily quantified grades and smiley faces and, in some cases, little gold, silver, yellow, red, or green foil stars that the teacher would have to lick before affixing to the page. In one fifth-grade classroom at Main Street School, dittos came back on very special occasions with little bleeps—googly-eyed colored cotton puffs with sticker-feet—attached. Other teachers used scratch-and-sniff stickers. Also pretty great.

Those kids who didn't live for rule following, both abstract and on dotted lines, learned to tolerate dittos and prayed they didn't lose them, because if they did, they were done for. Nobody had a copy machine. You couldn't just print out another. Crumpled or torn dittos were frowned upon. If you left one at home altogether, you were stuck.

45

SENIORITY

As you got older and scaled the corporate ladder, you grew more seasoned—wiser, experienced, the kind of person who reeled off charming anecdotes from times gone by and was capable of offering substantive advice—until you became the person people wanted to listen to even as they feared never getting the chance. Achieving seniority was one of the inevitable progressions that followed years of paying your dues. It was your turn.

But until you got there, when it was not your turn, you had to deal with the people whose turn it was, and they were untouchable. The corporate elder statesman was sealed behind closed doors or on another line. You weren't allowed to speak to him without an appointment made by his secretary and there were no appointments available, should you dare ask. Such hierarchical standards trickled down the organization. In any company, the chief executive officer outranked everyone just as at war, a general ruled over the enlisted soldiers and at home, parents ruled over kids. The associate marketing manager could pull rank on the assistant marketing manager, but if the senior marketing manager walked in, nothing of what either of those two proles said mattered much at all. Often it felt like you weren't allowed to speak—or, at the very least, you weren't encouraged to.

The Internet has collapsed these once painstakingly maintained distinctions, visible or invisible but always understood. The corporate gatekeepers—the executive assistants, the agents, the managers, the deciders—no longer stand between you and your überboss, just as there's no one between you and John Legend and Joe Biden, at least online. You can @ them. DM them. Publicly comment on what they say. Not much insulates them in an environment where you yourself can be a celebrity and an authority, at least for a micro–news cycle, thanks to one successful TikTok.

Online, the youngs are always at least three steps ahead, and their parents, teachers, and bosses know it. The whole adult world has to defer to the students, kids, and entry-level associates for tech tips and the latest terminology. On Slack, everyone is in the same typeface; bosses and new hires commingle in millennial lowercase-speak without the slightest nod to the org chart. If anything, the bosses are at a disadvantage: The older you are, the more punctuation you use. You're probably not even in the right channel; the cool kids in the department have all congregated elsewhere. While there, they can band together, they can organize, they can campaign and sign letters and post them on channels and sites the bigwigs have never heard of. It's not so much that you are untouchable as it is that no one wants to touch you.

That's a bummer for the higher-ups, but if you are young and ambitious, you can say things on the intraoffice messaging system that you'd never get to say in person to your boss's boss, let alone to your boss. If you came of age in the olden order, that may strike you as impertinent. But think what it can mean to those who get to be in the room where it happens with the person who is three titles above them, and to have that person hear what they have to say.

46

LOOKING OUT THE WINDOW

In the seventies, kids had nothing to do in the way back of the station wagon, the carbon monoxide seeping through the floor into cigarette smoke–laced air, uncut by air conditioning. Forcibly exposed to whatever terrible music your parents were into at the time, you looked out the window to remind yourself there was somewhere else. You looked out the window to watch the scenery. You counted mile indicators or wove your eyes in and out of the dashes between lanes while you thought about where you were going. The alternative was playing car bingo on those square game boards or Ghost or Geography with your siblings, assuming you were on speaking terms.

But people no longer stare out the window, not even when they are at the wheel. Everyone in the car, passenger and driver alike, is looking at something far more interesting, even if only out of the corner of an eye, on the mounted phone poking out from the air-conditioning vents or balanced on a thigh or on the built-in dashboard smart screen, displaying an array of podcast preferences and the GPS. They're glancing at their Apple watch, rotating an arm while keeping a hand on the wheel, eyes off the road just for a split second. Often the driver is bored because no one else in the car will talk to him. The person in the passenger seat is busy, busy, busy on her phone and does not care to be interrupted. In the back seat, the kids are quiet and content with their respective gizmos. Nobody is asking to sit by the window, which does nothing but cause an annoying glare on their screen.

Sometimes you can't look out the window even when you want to, even when there's a magnificent view, even when you're thirty thousand feet in the air. Airlines no longer put up the pretense of expecting passengers to gaze at the clouds, instead announcing at takeoff that shades must remain closed for the duration in order to preserve the viewing experience of fellow passengers. The *screen* viewing experience, that is. Have you ever flown over Greenland and dared peer at its calving glaciers by raising the shade an inch, or peeked out to see if you're nearing home, or looked outside nervously during turbulence? You get nothing but dirty looks and deep sighs; don't you know there's a satellite-fueled digitally displayed map in front of you for that?

And just try staring out a train window without the reflection of the TV show on the screen of the guy sitting next to you refocusing your eyeballs from the flowing river outside to the full-throttle action happening on Netflix. The restless brain can't help ditching the slow passage of landscape for the quick cuts of a thriller. We don't always get to choose where to direct our gaze.

47

TV GUIDE

In 1948, the silent film goddess Gloria Swanson appeared on the cover of the first issue of *TV Guide*, then a local New York publication known as *The TeleVision Guide*, heralding the emergence of a new medium and the dawn of a cultural era. This new magazine, a combination of breezy pop culture coverage and practical information about what was on when, was an immediate runaway success. Who didn't want to know what was on? By 1953, the magazine had gone national, its first all-American cover featuring Lucille Ball and her baby son, Desi Arnaz, Jr. *TV Guide* was the *Reader's Digest* of the pop-culture zeitgeist—news-you-can-use and couldn't get anywhere else, and yet small enough to sneak into the bathroom. Everyone seemed to read it or at least look at it on the supermarket checkout line.

By 1988, *TV Guide* was so successful that its purchase by News Corporation for $3 billion marked the most expensive publication transaction of its time. Barreling into the 1990s, the magazine published roughly 150 different editions tailored to regional markets, and included local listings in addition to national programming. Its elaborate coding systems evolved to capture the complexities of cable offerings in a given market.

Your local paper printed only the daily schedule; *TV*

Guide gave you the full week ahead with episode synopses. You could plan dinners around it. You knew when to park the kids in front of the TV and have a night out. Reading *TV Guide*—even, for us nonsubscribers, just seeing what was on the cover each week—made you feel you were somehow part of the same cultural tableau as the rest of the country, which together formed a once semicoherent quilt of passions, whether it was *Jeopardy!* or *Oprah,* one that has since split off into a zillion threads for a fractured nation. Now it's all on tvguide.com, but who looks there when a zillion other websites show the exact same thing?

48

CIVILITY

Goodbye, dear. Actually, goodbye "dear." This auntie-scented nicety of a word, the one that used to signal the beginning of any decent-minded letter, has been lopped off the top of emails, texts, Slack conversations, and other online correspondence, just as atavistic epistolary sign-offs like "Best," "Sincerely," and "Yours" no longer wrap things up at the end. So, too, go our titles and our given names, a waste of precious thumbwork. (Who else would be reading it?) The utility-minded Internet weeds out the extraneous.

With those lost words of personal acknowledgment and endearment, we also lose the insulating effects of kindness and—forgive the old-fashioned term—civility, two virtues that were already in jeopardy, victims of the increase in partisanship and the general coarsening of culture. Our online lingo, with its casual-to-dismissive terminologies, not only reflects that decline but also pushes it not-so-gently along.

It's easy to lose your manners online. People who would at least hesitate before yelling at their kid in person quickly resort to the ALL CAPS version in text (ARE YOU THERE!?! ANSWER ME!). Colleagues who have never met in person feel free to unleash on one another in a "private" channel. Have you ever been spoken to more viciously than you have on social media or been so vigorously upbraided for the merest of slights? It's not just everyone else; let's be honest, it's us, too. Even within the confines of a text, have you sarcastically responded to someone else in a way you'd never dare to in person? You have.

Among the unhappiest workers in the Internet economy—and between the Uber drivers and food app delivery people and the warehouse managers, the competition is stiff—are the comment moderators. Imagine being forced to tune in to this negativity all day: the attacks, the complaints, the loaded encounters and threats, not only from dedicated trolls but also from the mentally unstable and from the people just having a crappy morning. They are exposed all day to everyone else's spleen. These employees describe burnout, depression, anxiety, and the ongoing toll of stress as the daily baseline of their jobs, interspersed with jolts of anomie, misanthropy, and indifference.

The Internet was never intended to work this way. It was supposed to open people up to self-expression and connection. It was supposed to allow people to show who they really were or, under the cloak of anonymity, to break free from who others expected them to be. The Internet was meant for strangers to exchange freely with one another and in good faith. In a speech at Davos in 1996, the late poet and cyberactivist John Perry Barlow said, "We are creating a world that all may enter without privilege or prejudice accorded by race, economic power, military force, or station of birth. We are creating a world where anyone, anywhere may express his or her beliefs, no matter how singular, without fear of being coerced into silence or conformity." The bitter irony is that rather than bring us together into any kind of Kumbaya, the fraught setting of the Internet pits us against one another.

49

RECEPTIONISTS

The word "receptionist" comes from the word "receive," and that's what the receptionists did. These women—and they were nearly always women—were hired for their manners and their disposition because they were the first person a guest would encounter on visiting an office, and so they were to reflect the ideals or values of those establishments. Receptionists welcomed the outside world; not only did they answer the phone (unlike a future in which callers land in a cold and generic voicemail system), they sat out front by the elevator bank, well dressed and ready to greet in-person visitors with a smile.

Having gatekeepers around was helpful and kind of nice. If you were a visitor, they'd let you know that you were expected and allow you to fish out a candy from an always-stocked dish on their desk, and they'd look the other way when you took two. They'd let the person you were seeing know you'd arrived and point to where you could find the bathroom. They offered a seat. They greeted the mailmen, the delivery boys, and the bike messengers by name.

In their place now are security systems synced to databases on laptops, keypads attuned to magnetized card keys, digital handprint pads for now but perhaps soon, a James Bondian eye scan, none of which usher in visitors with so much as a "Hello." Because there are no humans at these entry points, the reception area—lounge, sofas, magazines, water—is smaller or nonexistent. It is no longer welcoming.

All the in-between people, the ones who helped negotiate these transitions, are disappearing. Sure, we don't strictly "need" these brief human-to-human interactions. We don't need all the clerks and secretaries and assorted helpers. In 2000, there were 124,000 travel agents in the United States. Within ten years, 43 percent of those travel agents were no longer. In place of human transcribers, Temi.com, Trint.com, and other online services use artificial intelligence to transcribe audio recordings, work that writers and editors used to do to supplement their paychecks.

With each of these abandoned posts, we've taken the "human" out of the interaction, subbing interpersonal interactions with digital ones. Pop-up windows manned by robots with human names (who decides between Calista and Omar?) cheerfully ask if they can help and then ignore us when we say "Yes." Who knows if there's even an algorithm behind the curtain? It's gotten all the harder to rage against the hapless 1-800-number customer service representative, releasing a week's pent-up frustration at the poor soul on the other end of the line. The automated system, should a phone-based service even exist now that there are Internet services like Jabber, doesn't care. But if you can find someone who prefers talking to an automated service over a human being when they are looking for help they are probably . . . not human.

50

PRIVATE OBSERVANCES

Nobody other than your family and close friends were expected to celebrate the holidays with you, and sometimes even they didn't care to join. Holidays—not the holiday party, mind you, but the actual day of observation itself—were a private matter; the rituals and ceremonies that might mean something sacred necessarily made them of limited interest to outsiders.

But the Internet unbinds us from formative religious and familial boundaries, and allows everyone to jump in, dressed for the occasion, even when it's not, strictly speaking, theirs. Pass that artfully filtered Passover plate, then scroll through everyone else's Easter ham and like it. You can celebrate Kwanzaa *and* enjoy the goofy Santa costume worn by one of your colleague's unidentified relatives. Heart your brother's ex-wife's second engagement because it might look weird if you didn't. Instagram the wedding using the suggested hashtag, allowing everyone to appreciate the occasion's good taste.

Social media helps us determine which holidays matter to us, fostering communities—or at least attempting to—that simulate that *It's a Wonderful Life* small-town experience. But it does take away some of the intimacy and informality of what was once understood to be a private moment. Think back to the mess of your family's get-togethers and imagine that everyone posted photos of that time you threw up on the living room carpet after eating all the chicken liver. Or imagine that a video of your grandmother's funeral had been somehow made public, broadcasting your first instance of true grief. Nobody beyond your immediate circle had to know about crazy Uncle Hal and his Thanksgiving poem or your ongoing struggle with Easter egg dye. Light the candles and join in lest you look like a Scrooge in front of the online everyone.

"Let's take a family picture!" no longer means recording the entire crew in weird matching sweaters destined strictly for Mom's family album. It means the photo will be made public.

On holidays, the thoughts and prayers that were once directed inward are now beamed out. Someone in your network urges you to pray for someone in theirs. Community events are virtual, bending our definition of IRL community to more closely resemble the virtual kind. Tune in to the latest Sunday mass if you didn't get to church on time; the minister will note your electronic presence there in the back. Welcome, distant relative and minor friend, elderly aunt and bedridden grandparent, drawn in virtually to an occasion they may otherwise have had to miss (possibly with relief). Perhaps you are happy to be included, perhaps you resent feeling like you must accept the invitation. Either way, there is no excuse not to show up.

51

LEAVING A MESSAGE

People just loved getting messages. It's true! When you got home at the end of the day, the number 4 or 6 flashing red on the answering machine felt like a winning scorecard. And no messages? Desolation. The standard "let the audience know this person is a loser" scene in movies featured a forlorn heroine or friendless hero returning from a night out to an answering machine bleating "You have *no* messages." The mechanical coldness of the voice delivering the verdict made it sound even more like a slight.

But not all messages were good. The messages could be from Mom. You could find out something on an answering machine only after it was Too Late, or overhear something you weren't supposed to, like a message from your girlfriend's secret lover. Entire story lines of books and movies were built around people hearing messages never intended for their ears; now, the story lines revolve around texts received, read, misread, or accidentally deleted.

Because the answering machine stood guard in this way, recording your own outgoing message was a big deal. Some people pretended not to care, others cared too much and changed their outgoing messages with some frequency, wacky one week and businesslike the next, waving a little sign of personality to the outside world that you could change at will, like a bad outfit.

Nobody bothers changing their outgoing message anymore because no one records one in the first place, not for their nonexistent answering machines and not for their voicemail either, and that's because they know nobody listens to it. We've collectively lost the code. Is it even worth punching in a password to listen to a three-hour-old voice say, "Call me" when you could glance at your missed call list and text back instead? On the smartphone, messages are rendered into a kind of nonsensical haiku by the hapless AI, the phone part being the one arena in which the smartphone isn't all that smart.

Well, good riddance to all that! No more of those one-sided convos from your best friend that went on for five minutes, seemingly about to wind up before launching into an "Oh, wait, there's one more thing I meant to tell you" as you held the receiver, forced to stay tuned lest you miss the one essential item. No more rewinding three times to make sure you got their phone number right. "Leaving a voicemail is practically an act of aggression," a novelist friend recently told me over lunch. "Expecting you to sit there and listen for a minute and forty seconds. Who *does* that?"

52

TOYS AND GAMES

E very year and only once a year, the Toys "R" Us Super Toy Run would give some insanely lucky kid the run of the store, letting him fill an entire shopping cart. Colorful rectangular boxes of Operation, Life, Risk. Stuffed animal after stuffed animal. Every *Star Wars* figurine on the market. Ovens that baked brownies that tasted like Play-Doh but were nonetheless profoundly desirable. You could hardly fathom what it would be like to win. But you imagine just enough to make you sick with envy of the inconceivable few who did.

"That Toys 'R' Us Time of Year," celebrated with its family of yuletide giraffes, has now permanently passed us by, along with Toys "R" Us and a good many toy stores. The kids have simply moved on, something to which adults, who still tear up helplessly at the opening sequence in *Toy Story 3*, haven't quite adjusted. The nostalgia editions of twentieth-century American board games sold in bookstores these days give off a whiff of desperation as parents try to recapture the halcyon days when "game" was a noun, not a verb. Remember us, these reissues of Clue and Sorry! seem to call out. Remember what it's like to make time for toys and games outside of chess championships, to invite a friend over after school to play Hungry Hungry Hippos before the little white balls all bounced off to their forever lost corners. Wrap us up and find us new homes at birthday parties; let us light up children's eyes with amazement and fill their afternoons with pleasure.

That's unlikely to recur. Kids seem more interested in watching other kids unwrap—or "unbox" as it's known on YouTube—toys than in coveting or playing with toys themselves. (One Australian unboxing creator, CKN Toys, is watched more than 460 million times a month.) Nor are toys the go-to gift anymore. By age nine or ten, kids no longer bring an assortment of colorfully wrapped boxes to birthday parties; instead they carry envelopes of prepaid gift cards for Amazon or Google Play or Apple. (Remember gift certificates—those oversized rectangles of stiff paper, calligraphed by hand with a colored fountain pen while you watched, wishing it could be for you rather than the birthday girl? You'd stand by mesmerized as the salesperson magically wrapped your purchase, even a gift certificate, curling the ribbons with the edge of a scissors in a way impossible to replicate at home.)

Most of the time, the iPad is the toy *and* the game. Online playdates (meeting in Minecraft, for example, or via Discord) are replacing physical ones.

Yesterday's kids, the ones who collected baseball cards and gathered for board games labeled "12 and up," have morphed into kids who scoff at "playing" anything other than videogames by the time they are eleven; they want to play what their parents are often playing. The new version of the Toy Run is a triple-digit amount of money loaded onto a gift card link that they can use to purchase "merch" from their preferred YouTubers and upgrades to their favorite games. Those grown-ups who still like to play analog games can rarely get the kids to join in.

MAPS

W ell before anyone could figure out how to refold it and put it away, the road map was gone for good. Sure, these maps would grow outdated soon after they were printed and would never reveal when a highway ramp was closed for construction. But they were what you could get when you crossed a state line and stopped at the gas station. You'd stuff them into the glove compartment or within the narrow side pockets of the driver's-side door, where they'd fade and tear over time and fly out the pocket the moment you opened the door on a windy day.

Now it's hard to find a physical map, never mind argue over the proper way to fold it. According to one recent survey, only 2 percent of Americans use road maps at all. Even among baby boomers, all of whom grew up asking tollbooth operators and gas station attendants for help deciphering embattled Rand McNally atlases, nearly half haven't consulted a paper map in over five years.

Kids were once taught to read maps starting in elementary school, coloring them in and, later, answering multiple-choice questions about continents and capitals. The annual unit on geography always began with a chapter on map literacy. Those kinds of maps were usually simple and dull, but a good map could drive the imagination. Now kids head to Google Earth.

EMPATHY

Given the extent of the communication pinging around—everyone having a voice and expressing themselves and being heard—you would think we'd all be linked arm in arm atop a shining pinnacle of peace, love, and understanding. Alas, the more people interact online, the less they seem to truly hear one another, and the less they *want* to hear one another. We may read other peoples' words and hear what they say, but we aren't understanding how they feel beyond, perhaps, how they make *us* feel.

That detached, depressed feeling that so many of us got during quarantine, when nearly all of us were reduced to online-only versions of ourselves, was only natural. When you're interacting with someone else online and it stays online, you *feel* the person you're communicating with less. When you don't get each other, the other person stays Other. They are flat.

You don't hear tone when words that feel laden with meaning show up as silent glyphs on a small screen, or read body language when all you see is FaceTime. Likes and hearts just don't carry the same emotional wallop as eye-to-eye contact, deep conversation, and full-body hugs. The bobbleheads projected onto a video call lose something without shared airspace, that ineffable way in which we connect with someone else in a physical setting even when no words are exchanged.

Oh, sure. Misunderstandings occurred all the time in the days when hand-delivered letters and calling cards were exchanged several times a day between the parlors of London in the 1890s, and lots of nuance got lost during those long phone calls with college friends in the 1990s. You couldn't see the person on the other end of the line rolling her eyes or be certain what it meant when your correspondent had signed "Sincerely" rather than "Most sincerely" this time around. But you did get a better sense when people were careful with their words in long, heartfelt letters, and people obeyed certain rules-of-the-phone.

What happens to this in the digital space? That the Internet ignores or undermines components of human existence such as empathy, deep relationships, child development, family harmony, sustained conversation, compromise, and compassion may be built into the system. Its products and services have been almost entirely developed by single, twentysomething men, whose motives, no matter how pure, are primarily based on money and power. The values reflected in online tools and websites don't generally take into account the priorities of a twelve-year-old girl or a seventy-five-year-old man, nor is artificial thinking based on the thoughts of those people. (Only 12 percent of leading machine-learning researchers—people who work in artificial intelligence—are women.) Some demographics just don't have a worthy impact on the bottom line. And not all feelings are moneymakers.

Empathy can now be filed, as are so many other essential features of being human (communication, friendship, violence), into two—often mutually exclusive—categories: real-world and virtual. The virtual kind tends to run shallow, as do the friendships, or what sociologists call "parasocial" friendships—relationships that exist purely in the mind and that are often one-sided, such as that between a fourteen-year-old and her favorite YouTuber, whom she'll message and buy merch from and have all kinds of unreciprocated feelings for.

And while virtual relationships can bind people together in their likes and affections, they tend to bind people against others in what they dislike and fear. Social media thrives on posts that grab attention, particularly emotional attention—with what's called "affective engagement"—and with emotions that are negative, primarily anger and fear, but also sadness and surprise, or, more bluntly, shock value.

People also tend to share posts that make them feel good and confirm their own beliefs, perpetuating what can become a closed circle of affirmation—the well-documented echo chamber of the web, rather than posts that explore other people's beliefs or ask others to do so. Rather than cross into others' emotional territory, we stay firmly within our own safe spaces. We repeatedly confirm our own biases rather than explore the other side.

In the online world, there is more speaking than hearing, and very little in the way of open listening. Interaction is more often about finding people to get angry with and angry at than it is about sharing hearts and minds. Basically, it's the opposite of empathy. On the Internet, fury does quite well for itself; it's the other feelings that get left out.

A 2010 University of Michigan study found that empathy among college students declined 40 percent between 1979 and 2010, with the steepest drops in perspective taking and empathetic concern taking place during the Internet era, that is, between 2000 and 2010. You may not be able to tie the decline of empathy to the vagaries of an algorithm in the neat terms of a scientific study, but it's nonetheless hard to ignore the coinciding trajectories.

55

HANDWRITTEN LETTERS

Who would throw away a personal letter? No one, not unless she was good and angry, and in that case, the letter would be burned, at least in the movies, where it would be tossed into an open fireplace or else lit by hand and held until the recipient's fingers nearly ignited with symbolic fury. Otherwise, letters were tidily folded back into their original envelopes and (if you were an organizer) tucked into files marked "Correspondence" or, at the very least, shoved into a shoebox or the bottom of a desk drawer. Postcards might spend some time affixed to the refrigerator first.

Instead of letters, will future biographers comb through Facebook feeds, Twitter threads, email chains, and collected texts? Is there any choice? These wide-open windows—filled with half-baked thoughts for the blogosphere or a thousand social media followers rather than an individual person, these updates written with an eye toward the number of retweets, rather than for sharing a private contemplation—may be the sole pathway into their subjects' feelings and thoughts, which is itself an impoverishing thought.

Think of the volumes of correspondence never to be published, and what we lose. Imagine not having the *Selected Letters of Ralph Ellison* to shed light on why the author never followed up *Invisible Man* with another novel in his lifetime. No fan mail from Charles Dickens to George Eliot, no exchanges between Henry James and Edith Wharton. No collected personal papers for the university library or academic archive, no packet of letters passed down from grandparent to grandchild, tied with a ribbon, and part of the family lore.

56

OLD TECH

Before the Internet, everyone in France had a Minitel. And what a marvel it was, an innovative object of technology almost universally embraced by the French, a people who don't necessarily welcome the new as a matter of national character. But between 1982 and 2012, Minitel (for *Médium interactif par numérisation d'information téléphonique*) had twenty million users across nine million terminals in France. The French were way ahead of Silicon Valley in this case; the Minitel was basically the Internet before the World Wide Web existed. And, because this was in France, every family was given one for free by the government, hooked up to a government-supported telephone line. French people couldn't understand how Americans weren't aware of the device; it was like not knowing about cheese.

The Minitel was an attractive little number, compact and tidy, but with access to everything. You could use its keyboard to play games or go shopping, read the news, chat with friends, and conduct bank transactions. You could check the weather and book a train. You could consult your horoscope and order takeout and bet on a horse. You could find a boyfriend through various dating services, and, inevitably, you could find a large trade in text-based pornography; ads for these were ubiquitous, covering public services in lewd promotions that were all prefaced with the same Minitel call number: 3615. Right away, Minitel use in the workplace soared. Though its graphics were rudimentary, as with the Internet, it was easy to lose track of time on it, which you had to reckon with when the phone bill came, inflated with hourly usage fees.

But by 2012, the Internet could do all the things the Minitel could do and vastly more, so France Telecom pulled the plug. Thus ended the model of a public, neutral, strongly regulated, and universally accessible networked system, without disparities in access or adoption, with a publicly run infrastructure and platform that offered privately run services—in other words, the kind of thing that would naturally occur in France and never in America. Like the Terminator of modern technologies, the Internet mercilessly obliterates tech that once seemed fabulously advanced but has worn out its utility or profitability, making what once felt like a well-paced march of time feel more like an Olympic sprint into the future.

Around the world, various defunct technologies of the pre- or early Internet have likewise been unplugged, each with their unique merits and particular deficiencies lost to the wind: Floppy disks in their stacked floppy disk containers. CRT monitors. America Online starter kits. Modems. Beepers. Pagers. Car phones. CD-ROMs. Thumb drives. Most of these are hardly missed, though witnessing the specter of a clunky car phone in an eighties action movie— nearly always signifying that a rich, callous swellhead (what kind of jerk thought he was so important he needed to be reached in his car?) has whizzed his way on-screen— still holds its charm. DVDs and their often-excellent director commentaries and bonus features got tossed into the bin alongside Blu-rays and CDs, or were at best siphoned into plastic sleeves inside an album that got put away in a cabinet. Your once-treasured wall of albums, the music collection you spent years accumulating, the one that showed everyone who entered your apartment who you were in a way that passing them your playlist never can, is now, yes, a playlist. The once almighty desktop computer itself, the one thing that kept you anchored to a particular workspace, is on deathwatch. In its place, a slender, portable laptop, which can be spirited away from one flex desk to another at any moment, easily replaced by another device and its human.

57

BEING IN THE MOMENT

There's something so powerful about being in the moment—and at the same moment as everyone else, whether it's marveling at a fireworks display or staring in horror as the World Trade Center burns or swaying to the final encore ballad at a stadium rock concert. It's that awed feeling when everyone is caught up in a sustained emotional experience, the air thrumming with the intensity of a large number of people ceding their boundaries to the energy of the crowd. It's that moment when you glance at the person next to you and share a look that conveys, "I get it. I'm with you. Isn't this something?"

Wherever you were was where you were, and no one outside of science fiction or a comic book could be in several places at once. That was impossible.

Yet when the Notre Dame Cathedral burned in 2018, few people in France stopped and stared, or paused to exchange expressions of mutual grief for anything more than a few seconds before reaching online. The vast majority saw it primarily through the lens of an upheld phone (as they filmed the flames and the smoke rising), or, their face tilted downward, on the phone in their palm, scrolling through other peoples' experiences, sharing with Maman in Briançon rather than with the person to their immediate right. Even the people who were actually there weren't entirely there.

Photographs of any gathered crowd feature this same phoneward gaze, whether it's the Women's March or a Billie Eilish concert. They are there but not there. Groups that used to gather to participate in an experience with everyone else there now gather to share their experience with everyone who is *not* there. One of the strangest phenomena to witness from outside was the way that during the January 6, 2021, storming of the Capitol by pro-Trump rioters, members of the mob regularly paused in the middle of the violent action to document and share the experience; will soldiers on the fields of the future stop to share wartime casualties as they occur? Imagine the trenches of World War I with selfies.

Full immersion doesn't happen in a group and it doesn't happen alone because while we are digitally present all the time, we are hardly ever fully present in the moment. Sure, there were always people who stopped in the middle of something to take a picture, at least those who had cameras on them. But now we *all* stop to take pictures. We stop to document with a text, a post, a short video, a story. We've learned how to fake that "wow, amazing" face. It's like we're all taking what are now called "plandids" or planned candid photos, if you can accept that such a concept exists.

It would be too easy to blame an absence of presence

on everyone else's endless notifications, but we aren't always the ones who are being disrupted: We disrupt ourselves—all the time, even if just for one quick second, a momentary glance at the screen. It's hard to stay present if you're also running through the full suite of photo-post-comment-share. You go running and, rather than lose yourself in the sheer exertion and the wind and the horizon, you know precisely where you are, how far you've run, the total number of footfalls, and whether you've burned off the calories from last night's Oreo binge. You are hooked up to Strava, where you can take in the cycling speed of your hypercompetitive cousin. Roughly one in five Americans use a fitness band of one sort or another and an additional 14 percent wear a smartwatch, devices that keep track of us as we keep track with them. With their help, you notice the start time, the progress, the goal, the end. Do you notice the trees?

We combat the effects of this inability to disengage with attempts at wellness and mindfulness, all of us desperately trying to reclaim some small portion of our own goddamn minds. Schools have introduced efforts to combat anxiety with group meditations, intermittent breathing exercises, and full days devoted to wellness, desperate to offset the jangle of screens. You can't blame grown-ups for trying to instill in their children what they've lost in themselves.

58

SPELLING

"Look it up in the dictionary!" Whether from the mouth of your sixth-grade teacher, your exasperated mother, or your exacting grandfather, this was one of the defining imperatives of adult privilege as viewed from the lowly stance of childhood. You suspected it was just what grown-ups said when they couldn't quite figure out how to spell or define a word themselves. "*You* look it up," you'd mutter under your breath.

Kids don't have to put up with this grievance anymore, because learning to spell in the Internet era is like insisting on doing manual arithmetic while holding a calculator. Besides, you know that if you're texting with two thumbs and ignore the autocorrects, your readers will ignore your errors, too. We've collectively decided to swallow those typos and decipher the thumb code instead. People understand that you're relying on Siri or voice transcription—it lets them off the hook, too.

When it really counts—in a school paper or work memo—you can right-click to the correct spelling and run it through spell check just in case; there's no risk of submitting a term paper riddled with typos. Who needs to take up desk space with a Merriam-Webster when you have a simplified version built into Google Workspace? The long-awaited third edition of the *Oxford English Dic-*

tionary will never see print; those who want the second edition from 1989 must settle for a used set online. Nor do kids today have to wonder if Roget's parents misspelled Roger, with synonyms now readily available in a drop-down menu. What's a thesaurus, anyway?

The appearance of new words and meanings and spellings in casual use is accelerating even as our grasp of more formal language and grammar withers away. According to linguists, words and expressions transmit faster across online networks to far-flung communities than they would in a close-knit village or even a cafeteria, where a "secret code word" might remain within the confines of one table of fourteen-year-old girls. People don't need to know one another in order to pick up language tics and inventive ways of expressing themselves, hashtagged or not.

For kids accustomed to speaking in emojis, the plain old words of conversation or novels may feel like a tired constraint. There's no way to duplicate an emoji in speech. There's no way to replicate a keysmash, when kids haphazardly smush their fingers against the keyboard to convey devastation, annoyance, or glee. The efficiency of acronyms like "lol" and "idk" or "brb" outpace the cumbersome spoken words they represent. Adding extra letters for emphasis like yesssss or heeeyy or nooooo may seem to replicate real speech, but in fact it's becoming a form of speech all its own. getting rid of capital letters shows you just don't care and that's cool. Kids tend to prefer this free-form to the rigid dictionary form of language anyway. Try it out sometime and imho, you'll see exactly what they mean.

59

RECORD ALBUMS

There was a whole delicious process to appreciating a brand-new record album, whether you got it at Tower Records or Merle's Record Rack or HMV. It was almost an act of religious devotion, from the admiration of the cover art to the slicing of the plastic wrap with a fingernail to the placement of the needle on the precise edge of its vinyl rim. You listened continuously all the way through before flipping to the B side, perhaps pausing to read the liner notes and lyrics, to search for a hidden track, to check out the photo inserts and absorb the look of the band. You'd waited years for this group's new album, and you wanted to luxuriate in the acquisition.

Unless you got off the sofa to relocate the needle into the next groove, there was no skipping songs, no shuffle, no allowing some invisible algorithmic entity to determine your next track. You wouldn't jump to the next song before the first one had ended, and there was no progress bar showing you had only forty-eight seconds left in the song anyway.

No, you sank into that sofa and listened to a full side. If you were doing this in the eighties, after you had absorbed it in its entirety several times over, you might pop in a blank cassette tape and copy it, while, if you didn't have an integrated stereo unit, praying that your mom didn't call you from another room at that very moment and screw up the whole recording.

You'd use your treasured album collection to make a mixtape, which took time and effort, curating a soundtrack that sent your crush the message, "This is who I am, and this is what I see you in." To give someone a mixtape was a genuine act of courtship, devotion, or friendship, and now it's gone. "Everything is being curated for me, so I don't need to be a curator anymore," one music devotee in his forties told me. "It's sad. Making a mix for someone else is so easy as to feel meaningless." Yet imagine finding the time today to listen to twelve to fourteen tracks straight through, in the order in which they were intended to be heard—it would take nothing short of an extraordinary feat of discipline.

60

WONDERING ABOUT THE WEATHER

The skies can no longer deliver an unexpected sunny afternoon or catch us without an umbrella. You don't have to check the morning paper or wait twenty-two minutes while 1010 WINS gives us the world before the weather. There's no mystery to it, no magical touch to the evening news's weathercaster, if you even bother to tune in to the evening news. You already know what the weather anchor is going to say.

With minute-by-minute changes in precipitation from light drizzle to a stormy mix, forecast ten days out by zip code, one is awash in a mesmerizing level of detail about one's current meteorological position at all times of the day. I have watched, stunned, as one of my kids fixated on the periodic bursts of simulated lightning that appear on the iPhone weather app while an actual thunderstorm with visible dramatic lightning raged just outside the window. In an office with all-window walls, people check their phones for the weather before craning a neck to look outside. I have glared in fury at the weather app when it dares contradict the weather around me. Betrayed.

We already know the weather at our in-laws' house in L.A., the forecast where we're traveling for work next week, and what kind of weather conditions to expect on our next vacation. Here are the slopes that are open. There's no excuse not to be prepared for every conceivable outcome. If you get caught in a downpour without a raincoat, it's nobody's fault but your own.

As for most freebie days off from school, there's no more wait, no more uncertainty, no desperate anticipation; children are never surprised when a snow day is called because they've been refreshing the Snow Day Calculator app and texting friends about it all night, and the school emailed that evening letting them know there was a strong possibility. Communication the day of the storm begins at five A.M. (why?!) when the school sends out a text, email, and voicemail to your cellphone and, if you are stupid enough to have a landline, that too, waking everyone up on the one weekday they can sleep in. At this point the only unknown is whether it's a two-hour delay or all-out cancellation.

61

BEDTIME READING

Some of us stubborn-minded people still need to read before bed, even if only for a page or two before passing out. We know how to prop up the pillows and elevate our book to the right height so that the bedside lamp's glow envelops the page. Sometimes we intend to lie there for hours and want all the accoutrements just so. And for those moments when one awakes at four A.M. and needs to be knocked out again fast, it helps to keep an especially tiresome or inscrutable book on the bed stand, and light that can be gently dimmed and tilted away from your sleeping partner.

Yet signs out there in the world mark people like us as a dying breed. Hipster hotels have phased out the bedside lamp, or if they still have one, it is there for design purposes only, not illumination. Its dull light is tethered to the table in such a position that it cannot quite reach the page. The real purpose of this outlet-encircled lamp is to recharge devices, not light up pages, a superfluous task when a tablet is lit from within. On a tablet, middle-aged eyes don't have to narrow worriedly at too-small text. No husband loudly turns the pages, annoying the spouse trying to sleep in the same bed; silent swipes scroll readers to where they need to go. The e-world reads in silent unison.

Nor do people still sneak print reading into the margins of their days. There are no hardcover books stashed in the bathroom; you can blame the iPad for making those visits suspiciously long. People don't routinely tuck paperbacks into their bags. Bedtime scrolling has replaced bedtime reading. Kids don't hide flashlights to read under the covers; they camp out there with phones. Nobody even keeps a flashlight by the bed anymore, because flashlights, too, are embedded in the phone. When there's a blackout, everyone runs around in a panic wondering whatever happened to all the flashlights.

62

THE EMERGENCY BREAKTHROUGH

D epending on your age and level of insecurity, whether you had something you had to say or something you needed to hear, getting a busy signal could be worse than missing a call altogether. Perhaps you were calling from a urine-infused phone booth, digging around in your purse for change, and despite pushing the coin return—inevitably temperamental—were forced to relinquish one of every three coins you poked into the rotary's greedy slot. Then you'd call the operator to demand that errant quarter back, or ask passing strangers if they had change, while ignoring the loudly sighing person waiting to use the phone next. You were stuck in there, staring at the graffiti scratched into the glass, the sleazy advertisements stickered everywhere, the mildewed leaves of the yellow pages tethered to the shelf below the machine. Had someone thrown up in there last night? Didn't matter. You simply had to get through.

That's because a busy signal meant that a conversation was going on without you, and if you were a teenager that meant—in your paranoid brain—that the conversation was surely *about* you. To confirm those fears, you could try phoning everyone who might be talking to the person you were trying to reach to see if you got the same ominous frog-like signal. Maybe it was just a mother's endless conversation? No. Two of your friends were definitely talking to each other, probably making plans without you. You'd dial both numbers again, circling each of the seven digits along the rotary dial, annoyed by the onerous eights and nines. Still busy!

This kind of situation called for the most powerful and perilous telecom maneuver of all, the emergency breakthrough. In the days before call-waiting, the emergency breakthrough was the one way you could get through to a friend talking to someone else on the phone. For a hefty charge, you could dial the operator and request that she barge into a call in progress and ask the respective parties to get off the phone—usually in cases of road disaster or medical trauma—so you could convey the kind of vital information that would save a life.

But you could also request an emergency breakthrough to save your social life, a drastic step that risked telegraphing an uncool desperation on your part. All of a sudden, in the middle of what was a private conversation, the operator's voice would interject: "You have an emergency breakthrough call from Lisa. Will you release the line?" Refusing to relinquish was a diss akin to being unceremoniously blocked or unfriended on someone else's social today. But usually people hurried off the phone, even if only to find out what was going on. Then it was on the interrupter to explain herself, to fabricate some kind of excuse that would place the blame on some other loser. Kids whose parents didn't go over the phone bill with a magnifying glass learned to abuse the service as a matter of course.

One more phone-based maneuver remained at the teenager's disposal—something so diabolical, it could only have been dreamed up by eighth graders. Taking advantage of a bug in conference call technology, you could dial two people at once and stay on the line while each person assumed the other had initiated the call. You plotted this out with care, choosing your victims to achieve maximum pain and embarrassment. One person could be the girl in math who never spoke; the other, the cutest boy in the grade. You could pair a girl on the outs with your clique with her unrequited crush. Hell, you could do it with any two kids you were eager to humiliate. Then you covered up the receiver to muffle your giggles while you and your friends listened to the awkwardness unfolding. Teenagers knew how to torture one another through technology long before the Internet rolled around.

YOUR ATTENTION SPAN

"Sorry, did you say something?"

"I *am* listening, just hold on one sec."

"I have no idea what I've been doing for the last hour."

"What was that thing I was looking up?"

"No, no, no, I *did* hear you. I swear. Just repeat that last part."

"I'm sorry, what were you saying?"

SLEEPAWAY CAMP

Your parents had no idea whether you loved sleepaway camp or hated it and it made no difference anyway. Sleepaway camp was a parent-free zone. You could eat Cocoa Puffs for breakfast. You could be the miserable kid confined to a lower bunk bed that everyone short-sheets or the girl who hangs out with a sleazy counselor from the boys' side. They didn't have a clue whether you were taking the swimming lessons you promised to take.

Your parents didn't know anything about camp that you didn't tell them in a letter hastily composed during enforced letter-writing time. Even if your parents were the types to send regular care packages or write every day, they were always at a snail mail's remove, incapable of catering to an immediate emotional need or asking where on earth you'd gone off to last night. For better or worse, going to sleepaway camp meant disappearing into the vortex.

Now parents know. They check the camp Facebook page and daily blog, and scroll through the day's photos on CampInTouch or Bunk1, using facial recognition technology to pinpoint their kids in the crowd at the talent show. They read the weekly update email from the counselor recounting the ins and outs of hobby day and pizza night. Drone videos record campers frolicking on the property and staff videographers beam out a steady stream.

All this lets parents keep tabs on their kids 24/7 while they're supposedly trying out "independent" living. Mom can text the head counselor. She can email her kids and then the camp owner if they don't reply. The camp may even allow phones in the bunk so that parents can say good night to their kids, all but tucking their sweetlings in. Those parents who don't want to know and don't want to worry and don't want to think about their kids for a few blissful weeks always have the option of "just checking in." And even they may find it awfully hard not to click on that update when an impressive photo of their kid on the trapeze is just a click away.

Some summer camps try to fend off this new together-apartness and maintain an old-fashioned parent-free summer, but it's an uphill battle. In 2011, one in ten camps allowed kids to use their devices, a number that tripled only two years later. Kids routinely sneak burner phones into camps that ban them, often at the behest of their parents, who don't want them to be unreachable. Camp directors learn to manage complaints from parents if their kids aren't able—or choose not—to respond. Some camps will scan kids' handwritten letters and email them as PDFs as a sop to parental requests. When the kids come home, they don't need to tell the rest of the family all about circus class and glass beading. Their parents were there the whole time.

65

RSVPS

Invitations, whether you sent or received one, used to be a big deal, and part of that was the invitation itself. There was so much potential in that folded rectangle of quality paper, with its fill-in lines for the name of the invitee. Going to the stationery store to pick out birthday invites, the power to decide between Star Wars or My Little Pony, was almost as exciting as the number of candles on your cake, a first step in the lead-up to the big day. Or maybe it was your Bat Mitzvah or Sweet Sixteen, and you'd ordered custom stationery, six weeks ahead of time, choosing between ivory or white and selecting turquoise blue for the calligrapher's ink.

Once the envelopes were licked shut and the mail collected, the wait began. "Did anyone reply today?" you'd ask your mom, contemplating the friend combinations among those coming and tallying the number of incoming presents in your head. If you'd gotten fancy, your invites would have included cute little RSVP cards, which arrived in a cascade leading up to the reply-by date. This state of anticipation, occasionally tempered by disappointments like the knowledge of a competing party or a cool kid's regrets, took up weeks of emotional energy.

Now the invitations are selected on Paperless Post or

Evite, and you may choose not to even bother with an RSVP date at all, given the cavalier "if I feel like it" approach people take to responding. Why doesn't anyone like to commit anymore? "I may or may not come" seems like the default position, whether it's a birthday party or a Wednesday two P.M. Zoom check-in at work. Those who do RSVP risk looking like they're trying too hard.

Is it that the stakes seem lower when both inviting and replying involve a mere tap on the keypad? Does it feel less important when you can see how many other people are also invited? Maybe the e-card landed in spam. Perhaps it's laziness or perhaps it's business, but an Evite can fall down the scroll of your in-box and into oblivion. People just do not respond.

Not so long ago, the idea of not replying at all—never mind replying late—was a strong rebuke, an unmistakable message from the foul depths of rudeness. I mean really, the request is quite clear: RSVP stands for *répondez s'il vous plaît*—"please reply"—and it's asking nicely. According to Emily Post, the code RSVP "has been around for a long time and it tells you that your host wants to know if you will attend. Reply promptly, within a day or two of receiving an invitation, and by the RSVP deadline at the latest, if one is given." Ms. Post offered clear directives about when and why it might be acceptable to switch a yes to a no (death, grave illness, similar) or a no to a yes (only when it won't upset the host's plans in any way). Above all, she noted, being a no-show is "unacceptable." Nowadays, it's standard.

In 2019, I received in the snail mail a tasteful invitation printed on heavy stock with an RSVP card tucked neatly inside, and a phone number to call if you opted not to mail the card in. Astonishingly, there was no email address included. My first thought was, "How quaint and unusual; most lovely!" but it was swiftly followed by, "What a pain." Manners are charming, but time-consuming.

66

THE SOCIAL STUDIES TEXTBOOK

In the 1990s, people got very worked up over backpacks. Hypercompetitive schools were piling homework onto the backs of millennial children, and their backpacks got correspondingly bigger and more elaborate. An article in *The New York Times* warned, "Heavy Backpacks Can Spell Chronic Back Pain for Children." The U.S. Consumer Product Safety Commission calculated that carrying a twelve-pound backpack back and forth from school and lifting it ten times a day put a cumulative load on children's bodies of 21,600 pounds, the equivalent of six cars, over the course of a single school year. Similar studies in countries like Spain and Italy echoed the alarm.

Parents were urged to sift through backpacks to make sure kids weren't lugging unnecessary items. Extra straps were affixed to distribute weight over fragile torsos. Roller backpacks modeled after flight attendant luggage were introduced to help keep kids' spindly backs from cracking under the burden. Oh, the shame of hauling one of those behind your sorry ass.

And then the weight lifted. Under President Obama, the Department of Education urged schools to convert to digital textbooks by 2017. Schools stopped ordering physical copies and upgraded to textbooks that weighed nothing at all. That moment at the beginning of the first day of school when books were handed out—if you were lucky you got one of the shiny new ones, maybe even an updated edition, but if you were unlucky you had to write your name on the inside back cover under the name of the student who had your bio textbook last year—was a thing of the past. No getting excited or annoyed about which upperclassman had your textbook before. No spending time trying to discern something about the previous owner by deciphering old doodles. High schoolers were told they could no longer bring the few remaining textbooks home but could consult them in class with teacher permission if they must.

And why should kids want to, given the high-tech alternatives that accompany their advance from secondary school to college? New low-cost, open-source textbooks online and an explosion in rentals via Amazon, Barnes & Noble, and other services offer options far less expensive than pricy hardcovers. Cheaper still are widely available pirated editions, which kids somehow never think of as thievery because heck, it's school.

In a 2019 op-ed in *The New York Times,* one college professor lamented that none of his students could locate the page number of a reference he made because they were all reading pirated versions. When he confronted them, explaining that this was in fact stealing from the author and the publisher, the students were confused. No number of antipiracy warnings had clued them in to the idea that pirating books—or movies or music or TV shows, for that matter—amounted to taking money from writers and artists. One in four college students admits to downloading free pirated textbooks themselves—or knowing someone who has. In the United States, the average money spent on material for college courses dropped from $701 per student in the 2007–8 academic year to $484 ten years later. Textbooks are just about the only aspect of college education that has gone *down* in price.

Students, noting the low value of textbooks, now rarely bother to procure them at all, if they are even assigned. One professor told me, "More and more students refuse to buy the textbook (more than 50 percent this semester), which seriously hobbles efforts to use them for class discussion." Instead of reading assigned chapters, students do the occasional targeted search for key passages, picking up scraps of information as needed for the midterm exam. In other classes, students delay purchasing textbooks until they see if they really "need" them.

For students who prefer print—and they do exist—up-to-date textbooks have become less available and even pricier. In fact, most people—even teenagers—prefer reading books in print to on-screen. There are advantages to the tried-and-true technology: Print textbooks don't freeze or shut down or fail to load. It's easier to track narratives in print, and to follow structure in complex material. Online, readers are more inclined to skim and scan, primed to swipe or click away or just quickly check one thing in another window. They control-F to search for a keyword they know will be on the test rather than slog through four long paragraphs. Far more readers multitask while reading on-screen than reading in print, 90 percent versus 1 percent, according to one survey of millennial readers. (Only 9 percent don't multitask either way, a hauntingly low statistic for those of us who write.) Think about trying to read a book while watching a TV show compared with reading on your phone doing the same thing. It's easier to toggle screens to an online story during a boring opening credits sequence you've watched twelve times before than to use the moment to dip into a novel.

It's no surprise that you absorb less when reading online, and not just because you tend to skim. In print, readers often memorize components according to how they appear in the layout—at the top of a chapter, near a subhead, on the corner of the page, indented dialogue. For those with a visually oriented mind, this mental image is especially helpful in committing material to memory. You rely on the geography of the page.

But the exigencies and imperatives of the textbook market can't help you with that. So you can bid farewell to that delicious brand-new textbook smell, the satisfying crack of the binding, the purposeful folding of corners, to pre-class shopping in the college bookstore, and to holding on to your college textbooks well into your thirties even if you never opened them again, a visual reminder of your college years. The bookshelves of the future will show no sign of students past.

67

VACATION

Oh, it was such a long time ago now—or at least it feels that way, who can remember—but back in the day, people used to get vacations. Vacations as in no work, not a phone call, not a text. A vacation in which you could leave home and work and obligations entirely behind for the duration. When you got back from one of those breaks, it was like parachuting in from a distant planet. Your co-workers wanted to know where on earth you'd been, your friends wanted to know how it was, your parents wanted to know that you were home safe. You wanted to hear all about what you'd missed.

If you ever got to have that vacation, it was surely decades ago. My last vacation offline—which is to say, my last vacation—was a January 2001 bike trip through Sicily. I didn't own a cellphone, a quirk that was just starting to be seen as an eccentricity, and for three whole weeks nobody heard a peep out of me and I was reachable by no one.

It feels impossible to even recapture the mindset in

which I could completely let go for three weeks, impossible not to sneak a peek at email even if just to wipe out the easy-to-delete ones that accumulate like fruit flies and peek at the important ones that land with the urgency of a ticking time bomb, so you know they won't explode in your face the second you return to work—a prospect daunting enough to ruin the vacation itself. If you didn't do the tiniest bit of in-box maintenance—it just takes a few seconds!—it wouldn't feel like a vacation. And of course you have to read your texts! It's not *really* work, you tell yourself. It's not vacation either.

We know this. According to a 2016 survey, almost two-thirds of Americans believe that periodically "unplugging" or taking a "digital detox" is important for their mental health. But only 28 percent of those who say this end up doing so. We unplug even less when we're on vacation because of course you're going to post photos and check that everyone enjoys your sunset cocktail. The idea of waiting until you get home to catch up, of inviting friends over a few weeks later to watch a slideshow, feels like asking them to enjoy a radio play or listen to records on the gramophone.

68

THE FILOFAX

On July 10, 2019, something happened that had not once happened in all my years as a paper-bound person: I lost my personal organizer, which in my case, is a Levenger Circa notebook I've settled on after much experimentation over the years with assorted Filofaxes and Dayrunners. I knew exactly where and how I lost it, shuffling it from one tote to another, alongside its supplementary companion, a Moleskine notebook in which I write down my daily tasks. It was there, and then it was gone.

And with that went my entire agenda—everything I had to do that day, all my meetings, a lunch, an after-work drink. I remembered most of it, because I'd given it a good once-over, as I did every morning, before we parted ways. The next day, however, was a near blank. The following week, a void. I'd had lunches planned almost daily; I just didn't know with whom or where. There were meetings I was meant to be in, some of which I'd convened myself. One of my kids was coming home from camp, I vaguely recalled, on which day was anyone's guess. With a gulp, I pictured the two unsent letters to two of my kids I'd tucked into one of the plastic pockets, along with my son's eyeglasses prescription, notes from several important conversations, a few keepsakes. All of it now lost.

This sorry situation had, of course, a solution, one that

has been embraced by many: convert to Google Calendar, Outlook, or any number of other electronic personal-information management systems (as they are known to the trade). You can instantly update. You can share your shopping list with your partner. You can sync and seam-lessly integrate personal and professional agendas. Every-one knows where you are and where you will be, when you're available and when you're not. In other words, your personal agenda is no longer strictly personal.

I, for one, would rather live a life of a thousand missed appointments. Only during the coronavirus pandemic did I find myself sending Google invites of necessity, attend-ing prearranged Zooms. All was nonetheless double en-tered into my companion Levenger. My new one.

Of course I went and bought another one—online—right away. Few retail shops sell such items anymore. In 2020, the mega-chain Papyrus went bankrupt. Mom-and-pop stationery stores have similarly shuttered. Filofax's pristine jewel-box shops, tucked into fancy retail stretches like the Rue des Francs-Bourgeois in Paris, have closed, as have its perches in high-end department stores like Saks Fifth Avenue.

Founded in 1921, the British Filofax (the name comes from "file of facts"), was described by *The Times* in 1987 as "an extraordinary saga of business success" for its ability to sell $30 worth of paper and unremarkable leather at a retail price of about $160. Back when there were yuppies, it was nicknamed "the yuppie handbook." During its hey-day, one devotee in Japan created *The Filofax Manual* to help newcomers acclimate. To own a Filofax was to be-come an adult of a certain amount of sophistication. You had places to go.

Back in paper times, printed calendars in multiple formats were a necessity. In 1981, the average household boasted four printed calendars. Most kitchens had a wall calendar affixed to a bulletin board (75 percent according to one study). Kids got a new calendar at Christmas, decorated according to his or her passion for puppies or Star Trek. Page-a-day calendars were a go-to stocking stuffer you could tailor to recipients' interests. In the office, massive desk calendars covered the wooden desks of the mighty busy, and the pinup or swimsuit calendar offered a casual reminder of occupational misogyny.

Much of our social and professional lives are determined by the systems we use to create them. A Google calendar can be shared with spouses and children and caregivers and extended family. Everyone is, quite literally, on the same page. Nobody can "forget" that they were supposed to be home for dinner at six. Both parties have a record of the updatable joint custody calendar. Mom knew about the late track meet.

Electronic calendar users ("normal people," my husband calls them) can be dismissive of their paper forebears. But let us note, for a moment, what paper offered: On paper, you can cross things out when you're done in a satisfying way that hitting delete doesn't deliver. On paper, meetings don't just "disappear" with no notice or "get moved" to a different week without anyone asking whether that's okay. On paper, you can affix Post-its, adding lists to your days and then peeling them off when the day's tasks are done. You can multitask within the same system, using pages in the back to store addresses, long-term goals, old doodles, and jotted notes. The accumulation of past annual inserts serves as a form of stand-in diary. A similar diary logged in the recesses of a hard drive feels decidedly less real and less yours.

Despite these advantages, paper calendars and their keepers have been put on notice. Those who don't keep their shared calendar regularly updated are considered suspicious. Paper hangs on by a paper clip.

69

EYE CONTACT

W alk into any place where people are gathered, and no one looks up to check you out. You don't get that glowy feeling when you can tell that people are happy to see you or you've been spotted by an old friend. You don't get instant feedback when you're having a good hair day or see that a dashing stranger is looking at you for just a moment too long and it might just be a flirtation.

Instead, everyone's gaze stays decidedly downward. Their phones and laptops and devices contain everything they want to see, and any peripheral movement probably isn't worth the interruption. We stare at our screens on the train platform, on the train, on the walk from the train to the office, inside the elevator, and for the rest of the day at our desk. Entire rides and walks and meals haze by in which nobody meets another person's eye, and those laughs and mutterings that erupt into the shared airspace are in reaction to something on screen, not to a physically present human being.

When we're walking down the street, our attention is elsewhere. Our ears are listening to a podcast on the AirPods hidden beneath our hair, and our eyes do not catch those of a stranger or a passing acquaintance because we are twalking (texting and walking; yes, that's a new word). We don't hear the whistle or catcall of a perfect stranger or the "Hey there" of a passing acquaintance. Twalking is neither easy nor safe, yet I do it all the time and apparently could get arrested for it. Cities like Honolulu are banning distracted walking, which is—no surprise—not safe. In 2018, pedestrian deaths reached a twenty-eight-year high. If we don't get killed doing this, we'll end up in physical therapy.

We may already be in PT to address the bent-neck carriage we're all developing; doctors fret about what this will do to growth in adolescence, to our posture over the course of a lifetime, to the future of late-life back and neck issues. One day, there'll be a whole generation of seriously bent-up old people hobbling around ignoring the skyline, twalking their way to the chiropractor.

Our most sustained eye contact probably travels via screen when people look at one another on FaceTime or in Zooms and Google meetings. Only when we're at this safe distance do we look people in the eye. Or at least it looks that way. For all you know, the person on the other side has another window open and is looking at something else altogether.

70

WORKING INDEPENDENTLY

D on't copy your neighbor's work. Come up with your own ideas. Trust your voice. Develop your own style. This was what you did in school unless you were forced into some kind of annual group project, a thing to be dreaded because someone always slacked off and one kid insisted everyone else follow his ideas. Otherwise, you would sign your name on the front page of your work and make it your own because school was where children learned to value their unique contributions, the fruits of their own labor and independent study. The resulting grade was either to your credit or all your fault.

But working on your own isn't the twenty-first-century way, and in any case, it's impossible, in a tech-forward high school, to say who wrote an English paper, whose science homework that is, and whether one particular student truly deserved a 92 on the take-home geometry test. Much of the work is done in shared Google Docs, and many kids do their work while on their phones with one another, trading answers back and forth via text. The theory is that these networked products and services help children learn valuable skills for the workplace: teamwork and collaboration. At the same time they deemphasize skills that might dampen the future bottom line of Big

Tech companies like Google, such as authorship (darned copyright and royalties).

And let's not kid ourselves: Collaboration has a rosy feel, but what it frequently means, as most students know, is cheating. The real group project? Covering up the fact that the popular kid in your group did zilch. Sharing answers and recycling projects from years past, while gussying them up to get past plagiarism-detection programs, is often a team effort.

Working together with one's peers also means constantly working toward consensus, which has an undeniable bright side. Yet at the same time, ideas that might be risky, unpopular, or idiosyncratic can be eased out by the watchful eyes of friends, classmates, and colleagues before they see the light of day. The oddball take can feel dangerous when it's subjected to peer approval. The personal essay, argument essay, or thought piece becomes something that you aren't just sharing with the teacher, but that you're subjecting first to your classmates. That means you need to think not just about what you think but also about what others will think of what you think. And that's scary. This prepares you for more of the same when you get to the office, and what were once closely held documents kept on a hard drive, perhaps outlining a personal version or a tough proposal, become widely shared works-in-progress on an open server, everyone hedging and agreeing until you arrive at some watered-down and voiceless compromise, the soft-scramble version of a proposal. Dissent is difficult under any circumstances, but especially under this circumstance, making it harder to learn and appreciate what it means to think for yourself.

71

MAGAZINES

There was a time, not so long ago, when people loved magazines, absolutely and truly adored them and gobbled them up, considering them a hobby and a habit and a personal and social and cultural and professional necessity. They looked forward to seeing who or what was on the cover, the sumptuous photographs and original illustrations, flipping madly through pages and pages of advertisements to get to the table of contents. Magazines were novel-thick and delicious; they filled the mailbox and were full of things to covet. You could purchase piles of magazines for a good long flight. You could gather them for free at the hair salon and go through the whole mass during an especially long color process.

September issues were the most rewarding, teeming with the year's best stories from the country's top writers and celebrated editors, justified by endless pages of ads, some of them dizzying with perfume strips. Walking with deliberate slowness past the newsstands that dotted every city block and airport gate, you'd crane your neck to see the defining stories of the week. In high school, I'd patrol the Upper West Side in search of the latest issues. The newsstand by the Seventy-ninth Street subway, just south of Zabar's, always had the earliest *Vanity Fair*, the first glossy to appear each month in what was a well-set order, swiftly followed by *Mademoiselle* and *Glamour*. Next came *Harper's Bazaar, Elle, Self, Cosmopolitan*, and finally, because they could make people wait, *Vogue*. The weeklies also arrived in a procession I knew well: Monday was for the competing covers of *Time* and *Newsweek*, *The New Yorker*, and *New York*; on Fridays, the high-low polarities of *The Economist* and *Us*. In between, there were *The Atlantic, Interview, Premiere, Paper, Spy, Harper's, GQ, Rolling Stone*, and, all too briefly, *George*. And when I was all done reading, I would put aside the best of them to be stored in reserved magazine files above my desk.

Each of us grew up in our own way on magazines, feeling rather pleased with ourselves and mature to find a fresh copy of *Boys' Life* or *Cricket* or *Young Miss* addressed to our own name in the mailbox, before graduating to *MAD* and *Seventeen* and *National Geographic*. Magazines we inhaled, reread, and shared with friends before we'd carefully take scissors to paper and cut pictures out, sometimes in silhouette, and affix them to our bedroom walls. A pretty good understanding of any twelve-year-old could be achieved by sweeping your eyes over the magazine pages adorning her room. Was it Ralph Macchio's puckered lips from the pages of *Tiger Beat* or a broody Simon Le Bon? Images of Metallica or action shots of the New York Rangers or muscled-up photos from fitness magazines?

By far the best perk at Time Inc., where I worked in the nineties, was the steady stream of free periodicals. Every day, a cart rolled around distributing the many-paged splendors of *Time, Fortune, Entertainment Weekly*, and *InStyle*, to all employees. On Friday afternoons all the office doors slammed shut at once when *People* arrived, as everyone turned to Star Tracks.

You could occupy a full afternoon reading a single issue. My friend Alysia and I spent an entire bus ride from New York to the Catskills dissecting a single copy of *Entertainment Weekly*'s legendary episode-by-episode guide to *Seinfeld*. We marked it up, circling episodes we wanted to see and laughing anew over the ones we had. What an amazing feat of research and service to provide readers with a bounty of otherwise unavailable information—who would have thought it possible? Someone got *paid* to put it together. Now it's accomplished by dozens if not hundreds of websites and obtainable with the stroke of a keyboard. The results are probably far more thorough than *EW*'s version and full of opinions it would never occur to me to have, but I never feel compelled to check any of them out. It's not the same without the immersive quality of that special-issue magazine experience, all that information culled and contained within two glossy covers.

72

ASKING POLITELY

It's "May I?" not "Can I?" Never repeat the request unless asked to. Never interrupt. Wait until the grown-ups have stopped talking. Most kids learned these rules from an early age. My brothers and I used to barrel through our backyard and down a brambled passage to the house around the corner, where we would ring the neighbor's doorbell, waiting a full minute before pushing it a second time: "May we please climb your tree?" we'd ask when the older couple who lived there answered, and then, eyes on the bowl on the coffee table, "May we please each have a piece of candy?" putting a polite veneer on what was essentially a home invasion.

The whole "May I?" versus "Can I?" distinction no longer applies when children today learn to ask for something they want because asking an Internet-enabled machine requires an altogether different language: If you don't tell the thing what to do in the clearest imperative possible, the thing won't listen, and small children do not like that. They learn to weed out excess words like "please." No hedging or "Would it be okay if . . ." or "I would like to . . ." Instead, it's:

"Alexa, play Beyoncé."

"Alexa, tell me the time."

"Siri, call Mom."

And the machine gives them what they ask for, faster than any human would, and without remonstrance, rebuttal, or complaint. In lieu of butterscotch candies and tree climbing, she offers targeted data and instant gratification.

73

AIRPLANE ENCOUNTERS

When hundreds of people packed themselves together into a flying metal box for hours, they were bound to interact. They'd comfort the unaccompanied minor asking nervous questions about takeoff. They'd check out the last-minute spinning-rack purchases that separate the Stephen King readers from the Danielle Steels and crane their necks in unison to watch the flight attendant's seatbelt demonstration at the front of the aisle. They'd eavesdrop on the couple in the row ahead (budding romance or deteriorating marriage?) and exchange furious glances with their neighbor in response to the kids' kicking from behind. When the shades were pulled down for the in-flight movie, they'd groan communally over the eastbound selection, a box office dud featuring a lovable hound. Passengers were in it together for the long haul.

Well, that's how it was. Now there is atomized silence on board. Eyes are fixed on individual screens, whether embedded in the seatback in front of them or propped up on a personal device. Passengers do all they can to teleport outta there; they use the airport Wi-Fi until the airplane taxis to the very last second of takeoff and then at ten thousand feet shift onto the airplane's Wi-Fi entertainment; cheaters never turn their own service off. They'll text their friends back down on earth via satellite rather than speak to the person squished up beside them for the next twelve hours. The plane might be hurtling toward its doom and rather than grab the hand of the person three inches away they'd be trying to send one last message to someone thirty thousand feet below.

There's little chance of meeting someone you'd never otherwise have met. It could have been a handsome stranger, a new friend, or a potential customer. It could have been someone whose polar-opposite political opinions you'd be hearing firsthand for the first time. On the plus side, now you're also spared the tedious conversation about your neighbor's sales conference and his personal take on the meal served the last time he flew. You, too, can focus on your own screen, undisturbed for the duration of the flight.

74

YOUR CHECKBOOK

Finally, a checkbook of your very own. This was a significant upgrade from a mere passbook, which meant you had only a basic savings account and had to fill out a form and stand in line for a bank teller in order to get money. A checkbook—only adults had checkbooks—meant financial independence; it meant you had access to money anywhere.

There was something terribly sophisticated about brandishing a checkbook, perhaps in a monogrammed leather holder, flipping to the appropriate page, and signing with a flourish. In school, you learned to balance your checkbook as part of the standard math curriculum. Every student got a lesson on checks, learning to only write "and" before the cents when spelling out the sum and to always sign your full name. One accidental scribble, you were told, and your check would be useless. Tearing up a precious check, which you had to order by mail, was a waste, though it could make for high drama in the right situation. There was something definitive in scribbling VOID across the front and ripping it into smithereens. Many a pivotal movie scene hinged on the tearful tearing up of a check, often clear down the middle, pieces falling to the floor. I simply refuse to pay! Or: Your money is no good to me. I cannot accept it!

Restaurants took checks, gas stations took checks, corner shops took checks. Anything you wanted to buy off a TV commercial took a check or money order (remember those?) sent by mail. Checks were the preferred alternative to the credit card, which was not quite real money and therefore potentially shady. Pull out a credit card to pay for a big-ticket item and the cashier would have to haul out the phone-book-sized compendium shipped to retail establishments every week, listing all the lost and stolen credit cards in tiny-type numeric order. Working at mall stores during high school, I dreaded searching for the latest edition among the outdated ones shoved under the counter, just as I dreaded a confrontation that might force me to demand that the customer hand over a purloined credit card. With a check, at most, you had to verify the name on the customer's driver's license.

Once accounting for 86 percent of all noncash purchases, peaking in 1995 when nearly fifty billion checks were written and signed, the check is now hardly acceptable at all. Between 2000 and 2012, the number of checks used dropped by half. Try to pay by check at a bodega and you'll be met with disbelief. Even little old ladies who paid by good honest checks their whole lives dare not attempt it now. Travelers' checks would baffle anyone under thirty. So, too, the notion of locating a foreign currency exchange or heading straight to the American Express office or visiting multiple kiosks to hunt down the best rate and lowest fee, long an essential ritual of international travel.

Currency itself is on the way out, with only 7 percent of all financial transactions involving bill and coin. The majestic bronze cash registers of yesteryear have been replaced with the sleek rectangular tablet guilting you into selecting an 18 percent or a 20 percent tip under the watch-ful eye of the kid who just handed you your mocha latte. With them go print receipts, now emailed directly with a tap of the touch screen. No more gathering bits of taxicab scroll or blurry restaurant tabs at tax time. Well before April 15, your online bank drops a summary of your ex-penses by spending category into your in-box. You don't even have to ask.

A growing number of stores accept only cards or mo-bile payment, which cuts down on the potential for theft and human error. Alas, those with a poor credit history and those who do not own a smartphone or credit card cannot partake. Until New York City banned cashless en-terprises as discriminatory and privacy invasive, it was al-most impossible to buy an overpriced cup of freshly blended juice with a crumpled bill. But many other cities both in the United States and around the world have con-tinued and expanded the cashless flow.

Even those of us who earn a steady paycheck hardly ever see the actual check, let alone endorse it and take it into a bank branch. If you do get a paper check rather than direct deposit, you can merely scan it in yourself, following the passage of a law in 2003. The check itself can then be tossed into the shredder. By 2007, roughly 40 percent of all checks were "electronified." It's hard to remember that going to the bank and waiting in line for the next teller was a weekly ritual as much as filling up the car with gas and buying groceries. People used to get to know their local bank tellers. When did you last even see one?

75

MISSING OUT

"You can't imagine."

"You had to be there."

"You don't know what you're missing."

Oh, but you can, and you weren't, and you do. The fear of missing out—FOMO as we now know it, that unsettling sense that something might be going on without you— has been replaced with the knowledge that something definitely *is* going on without you.

It was dreadful enough not to be invited to a party when you were in high school. But to know very well that the party carried along just fine without your presence is far worse. Instead of overhearing in the school hallway Monday morning about a beach bonfire last Friday night, kids today know all about it while it's raging, seeing it pass them by in boisterous but fleeting snaps from the dejected vantage point of their living room. When the coronavirus quarantine forced everyone to stay home, it was almost a relief for those kids who were regularly sidelined; now everyone was in the same houseboat.

It's bad enough for the adult who is almost forced to monitor exciting things they aren't participating in. Imagine what it's like during the excruciating span of adolescence, when, no matter how many friends you have, part of you always feels uncertain about your place in the pecking order. For teenagers, social media *is* social life. If they don't want to miss out, they have to keep up, and that is now a ton of work. They have to monitor Internet comings and goings with vigilance and discipline. They have to be the last person to leave the Houseparty and hold tight to the Snapstreak, in which a designated group has to post daily for days on end.

Those junior-high feelings don't necessarily dissipate with the Snaps. We all know the experience of going online to find some widespread—at least widespread within your silo—exchange ricocheting around, perhaps pegged to a phrase ("pink kitten") or hashtag (#killhernow) that everyone except you seems to get and find hilarious/infuriating/crazy. At any given moment, a "conversation" is taking place, while you were sleeping, having dinner with your kids, or having the gumption to run an Internet-free errand—and it's too late now. At least you can see exactly what you missed.

76

PENMANSHIP

I n sixth grade I got an "unsatisfactory"—the dour euphemism for an F at Main Street School—in penmanship on my report card. My lowercase "h" did not begin, as it should have, from the bottom, but started instead with a top curlicue, an approach I'd perfected in my efforts to develop a signature style, an extravagance that didn't fly with Miss Harper.

None of my kids have known the pain of an "unsatisfactory" in penmanship and not because their handwriting is particularly good, but because penmanship is no longer considered worthy of grading at all. The Common Core curriculum emphasizes legible handwriting only for kindergarteners and first graders before toggling over to keyboard instruction. The moment children have grasped basic lettering, iPads are passed out, as early as preschool, giving kids little time to master the techniques of what was once considered acceptable handwriting.

When a ten-year-old boy from New Jersey won a national contest in cursive in 2019, his feat didn't elicit the reaction one would have expected a generation ago: marveling at the ability of a child so young to excel at a skill that typically requires years to perfect. The reaction was shock that such a contest even existed.

Mention "script," the shorthand for cursive, to a sixth

grader today and he'll assume you mean a computer script, which generates webpages, or maybe the script for a TV series. He might confuse it with shorthand, also practically left for dead on the paper-strewn floor. At the Library of Congress, where volunteers are recruited to input old documents into the permanent digitized record, the younger staff has to be paired with those from older generations because they can no longer read cursive at all.

Along with the abandonment of cursive comes the waning of the signature. When asked to sign a document, the average teenager is stupefied. What was once a necessity of adult life has been phased out as cashiers, formerly trained to check the signature on the back of the credit card to make sure it matched the receipt, ignore whatever scribble lands on the touch pad. DocuSign allows a signatory to input a finger-drawn signature on a touch pad and then auto-fills it throughout a document. You don't even get the practice.

While some see handwriting as antiquated, there are benefits to forming legible sentences by hand, and not just for the development of fine motor skills. Studies show a connection between the linked letters of cursive writing and spelling proficiency. (Then again, who needs spelling?) Other studies show that cursive prepares the brain for reading and writing composition. People demonstrably learn more when they put pencil to paper than when they swipe a screen. In 2019, after Baltimore County implemented a 1-to-1 laptop per student program, with textbooks, paper, pencil, and pens disappearing from the classroom, grades dropped across the board. A 2012 study of the brain scans of young children as they typed letters, traced them, and wrote them freehand found that only when children handwrote letters did the scans show the same activity in the brain that activate when adults engage in reading and writing. Kids both absorb and retain information better while writing by hand than they do when tapping on a screen. There's a reason you were always told to "write this down carefully." Writing things down was how we learned.

"EXCUSE ME"

Go ahead and say "Excuse me" as often as you like, but nobody will notice. They're too busy. They're listening to a podcast. They're deeply absorbed in their group chat, and you cannot break through that hyperfocus with a mere apology. They're caught up in something beamed into their ears via earbuds hidden under their hair or hat. There's no need to say you're sorry or "Pardon me" or any other nicety when you bump into someone because it just doesn't register, and you'll get scowled at in any case. We can save the bother yet stay bothered.

CHRISTMAS LETTERS

A lot of work to write, very long to read. Everyone already knows what's in there anyway.

FIGURING OUT WHO THAT ACTOR IS

Nothing would distract me from the plot of a movie like trying to figure out who the hell that actor was and coming up with a total blank. I'd know I knew him from somewhere, but damned if I could figure out where, and it didn't matter that it didn't matter. It mattered to me! But I had to sit on the conundrum in the theater for two long hours, unwilling to whisper the question to the person next to me for fear of being shushed and losing a snippet of crucial dialogue in the process.

Now it matters to my kids, too. Watching the latest Marvel movie, they'll do what everyone else does when they can't immediately name the other movie they saw the bad guy's henchman in; they'll google. They'll IMDb them or check Wikipedia. Watching a movie at home without a phone in the room is like a deliberate provocation. Why live with that frustration? Why suffer the mystery?

PASSING NOTES

There were the notes you took in class and then there were the notes you wrote on the ripped-off corners of those pages and passed around to your friends in class. Two very different things. Those latter notes were the ones that gave the more accurate picture of what was going on in school. All the turmoil, giddiness, rejection, and constant, tortured manipulation that characterized the complex lives of girls during that middle zone between childhood and adolescence showed up in those crumpled pieces of loose-leaf. They were so important, you were willing to pass them at considerable risk. One clumsily passed note dropped on the floor and you could get in serious trouble or, at the very least—and this was bad enough—suffer brutal embarrassment when a teacher or other unintended recipient intercepted. The idea of posting these notes where others could see them was inconceivable.

In a pre-texting, pre–social media world, notes were how we navigated the intricate networks of friendship, how we got through dull classes and made plans for what to do once released at the end of the school day. Notes helped us discern our allies and enemies. Putting fleeting fury and petty grievances into words on paper that could somehow make their way into the wrong hands launched many a middle-school feud. Because these missives were considered *private*.

At the end of a tumultuous, intermittently torturous eighth grade, a period that seemed to stretch over a good four years, my best friend Ericka and I gathered our notes and did something you were never supposed to do: We shared our respective caches of folded-up squares (remember how you'd write the recipient's name on the outside?). I read her notes and she went over mine, and we discovered something that teenagers were traditionally protected from: what other people, our supposed friends, said behind our backs. Ericka had assumed that our friends only bad-mouthed me to her, and I'd assumed the same of her. In fact, we were both targeted, used, and lied to. These discoveries were so devastating, we cut off ties with the rest of our friend group and started out anew in high school.

Lesson learned, we put our notes away. But I've kept mine ever since, sorted into a brown accordion file, the kind you close with a string that loops in figure eights around two metal circular fixtures. It sits in a large plastic bin in the basement, evidence not only of my own petty past but of an entire lost form of social life.

81

SICK DAYS

Y ou wake up with that sore throat, achiness, and what feels a lot like a fever. You didn't get enough sleep and are surely coming down with something. Or maybe you just wake up feeling crappy and don't want to go to work. Relax, take a sick day. Here's what it will look like:

You'll grab your device and ping your supervisor to let her know you simply cannot come in. You'll scroll through overnight emails. You'll write up an out-of-office autoreply and change your Slack status to sick-face in order to minimize the notifications—but that won't stop you from responding to the most urgent messages, no matter how feverish you might be. If you don't, you'll fall behind.

In other words, it's not really a sick day.

Even those who came down with a serious bout of coronavirus during the pandemic made sure to send a group update and coordinate regular check-ins with co-workers— this is part of the job. You may be out, but you are reachable, "away" but still tethered to home base. It is almost criminal—at the very least, arrogant—to suggest you will be completely inaccessible. Unless you're on a ventilator, you're always answerable to someone.

If you are old enough to have had one, you'll remember the old sick day well. After leaving a croaky phone message for your boss before she came in, you crawled back into bed and slept for a few hours only to wake up for some toast before retreating back under the covers. You were oblivious to whatever was going on in the office and were grateful for it. You had no clue what letters may have arrived in the mail, what phone messages were left, what happened during the meetings you missed, and that was fine. Nobody would hold it against you if you needed a few days to catch up upon your return. You were *sick*, after all.

You're not allowed to be sick like that anymore. Nobody gets to, not the lowlings nor the almighty honchos. The concept of a sick day has fallen away as naturally as the concept of the workday itself. There can be no "after work" when the workday has no end. Seven in ten adults say they use their phone for after-hours work, and probably more would cop to it if they were truthful—or if they realized that even those efficient deletes of nonessential work email count as work. In France, land of early retirement, generous pensions, and labor strikes, the "right to disconnect" went into effect in 2017, giving employees the right to ignore their boss's emails after hours. Who can imagine such a thing ever happening in the United States? It's enough to make you sick.

SECRETS

Modern procedurals inevitably contain the scene where the detective calls in the techies to scan the victim's or suspected perp's hard drive. Even if the bad guys had the foresight to wipe their computers clean, the truth will out. Secrets are not hidden in a bottom drawer or a safe-deposit box. They aren't whispered to a single person on one's deathbed or written in invisible ink on the back of a will or secreted into a locked diary. The secrets are on our laptops.

It didn't take long for us to realize that what we thought our personal corners of the cloud or the ancient histories of our search engines weren't secret at all. The terrible truths we've tried to hide from the rest of the world are findable in that one email or that "private" message sent on Instagram or the text we thought we'd deleted. Perhaps someone on the other side did not delete. Someone on one of the many other sides took a screenshot, a photo, or a full-length video. Even if it was erased it can be retrieved. Whatever was said or done has been caught.

Like some witchy seductress, the Internet spirits our secrets out of us and then reveals them. We can find out other peoples' secrets as easily as others can find ours, and we are all insatiable snoops. When every secret can be uncovered, we come to live in dread of our own curiosity.

CARD CATALOGS

With their indecipherable series of numbers and inadvertently amusing plot summaries, card catalogs were as likely to lead you astray as they were to direct you to the book you needed. At some point in elementary school or junior high, the librarian attempted to instruct you on the inscrutable Dewey decimal system. Without a master's degree in library sciences, most people kind of fumbled through.

But what fun that fumbling could be! I could spend hours flipping through those oversized hunks of furniture, marveling at the contents of each card: the absurd books on obscure topics that people insisted on writing and the mystery of why there were three copies of a particular ornithology book, each with a slightly different entry. Outdated books from the ancient times, all wonders of the public library.

The only card catalogs you'll find now are on eBay—and they're empty. You can also find the old library editions of familiar books from the days before electronic checkout, when a checkout card at the back of the book had to be retrieved from its vertical envelope and stamped with a smudged due date. These were the days when you had to trek to the library, search through the card catalog, and then venture into the stacks to see if a book was in fact there. Now you reserve the book online and get email noti-fications when your name comes up on a waiting list. No more adventures in the stacks, where you might never find the book you were looking for but might instead find something even better.

84

THE COLLEGE LECTURE

Pity the poor professor standing before a lecture hall today. Students do not stare up at the stage, rapt, but at their raised laptop screens. No matter how loudly the professor raises her voice over the thrum of keyboards, she cannot gauge student interest by eye contact or facial expression. Without pencils poised, there's no way to judge who is engaged and responsive; the patter of keyboards could mean that those students with furrowed brows in the third row are just texting one another. This isn't paranoia. One study that took a screen capture of college students' laptops every five seconds found that students switch windows and tasks every nineteen seconds on average, all while in class.

The number of students gathered at a lecture no longer bears any relationship to the number of students enrolled, even taking into account those who overslept that morning. An incalculable number simply don't attend at all, ever, even if they claim to be interested and aim to do well. Many students just wait for the PowerPoint, that much-despised tool of marketing managers and sales directors, which professors are now expected to create and post for each lesson not only for students who missed class but also for the students who were there but not there. "An invasive species," one professor calls it.

Because kids no longer handwrite anything in school, by the time they get to college, they have no concept of note-taking. As one professor told me, "I have explained to my college Western Civ class that PowerPoint, which are the teacher's notes, is not the right way to go, that studies have shown they need to take their own notes, and in handwriting. I lecture in a reasonably lively way, but with the sure sense that some students wish I would shut up and just show videos and arrange classroom games instead." When the professor was a student, he said of one "brilliant" professor, "We considered ourselves privileged to take notes when he spoke." Now, he says, students have stopped taking notes altogether. Forming the letters takes far too long, and they have no idea where to begin, making lectures a less effective way to learn.

No wonder so many students skip lecture: They can attend virtually or grab it online later. One day they may no longer have a choice.

85

MEMORY

Do you remember when we used to hold on to basic facts and daily obligations? All by ourselves? Without a single pop-up reminder? Not anymore. We've given up the job of remembering anything on our own and left our memories to the cloud.

Creating a new memory involved observing things using our full attention as they happened. It meant writing things down by hand, collecting, sorting, and shelving. Creating a long-term memory, in this earlier, brain-based system, required the absorption and retention of factual detail, conceptual comprehension, and syntheses. You constructed these memories and then slept on them overnight, and a good portion of them still remained in the morning. There was information that you were regularly forced by circumstance to recall—your bank account number, your locker combination, your parents' anniversary—without visual assistance. You used your mind's eye.

But we no longer give our brains those regular workouts, not that we thought of them that way at the time. It was just what you did from an early age, starting in preschool. We don't bother memorizing things like poems or the first forty digits of pi, the capital of Utah and the seven times table. Storing this bank of cultural knowledge was a signifier of adulthood and of a fine education, if not necessarily a sign of intelligence, but now it's all online. Open-book exams, a rarity during my schooldays, have become a regular feature of secondary school education because there's little point to teaching kids to memorize for a test when the computer retains the information with more efficiency. Kids learn there's no point.

Do we continue to create organic memories the old-fashioned way? Mostly not. Taking a picture with your Samsung Galaxy or cutting and pasting addresses into your contacts doesn't have the same effect as entering them in your little black book. Are the memories of what we've seen with our own eyes swiftly replaced by the digital memories we scroll through repeatedly afterward? They are. We may all suffer from the photo-taking impairment effect, in which memories are externalized, rather than internalized, meaning they never become long-term memories of the original experience, associated in our brains with smell, tactile experience, and emotion. This updated process is referred to as cognitive offloading: We don't need to remember anymore, and so we don't. It sounds relaxing, and for many people, it can be.

With cognitive offloading, our remaining capacity to remember and our way of remembering shift. It isn't just that our memories are getting worse—though they are—but that they are also changing both in terms of how they are formed and how they are maintained. They are changing in the *way* they change over time. When we capture our lives on Snapchat and through Instagram stories, where they are briefly recorded, then vaporized, we may wind up recalling the recording of the moment and the reaction to the moment more than we remember the moment itself. According to Daniel Schacter, a professor of psychology at Harvard, research shows that "reactivating an experience after it occurs can have large effects on subsequent memory for that experience and, depending on what elements of an experience are reactivated, can even change the original memory." We don't quite know what these new mediated memories mean, or what they will have replaced, but someday we will find out—assuming we remember to check.

One morning, rushing to the office, my mind chasing after a dozen things I needed to do that day, I got a notification on my phone: "You have a new memory," it said. Out of nowhere a photo I'd taken on a trip to Australia for a book festival in 2017 popped up. Why now? I wondered. I clicked on the notification. Something in the algorithm must have told the Internet I needed to see images of the Sydney Harbor waterfront. Perhaps it was entirely random. I would never have thought of that particular view at this particular moment of all moments. Only one thing I knew for sure: I had a new memory.

86

MOVIE THEATERS

On Thursday nights, a ladder would appear in front of the movie theater on Main Street, marking the start of the weekend. You could watch the guy manually insert letters onto the marquee, trying to guess whether the "B" would mean *Back to the Future* or *The Breakfast Club*. And you needed to know because that theater was the only place to see either one, sitting in a darkened room, the designated space for movie viewing, alongside your companions and a packed room of strangers, eating overpriced Twizzlers and faux-buttered popcorn. Friday nights, when new movies opened, were the most exciting night of the week in many a small town and big city.

If you didn't happen to drive by the theater Thursday night, you'd have to wait for the local listings to be printed to find out what was playing. Long lines for tickets were an understood part of the movies. You lined up for tickets and you lined up for seats; nobody got to pick their spot online a week ahead of time. When *The Phantom Menace* came to

San Francisco in 1999, fans lined up and camped out for a week. A whole society of die-hard *Star Wars* fans got their own extended street party. Beginning in 1989, you could also call 777-FILM for Moviefone, which allowed you to punch in numbers—assuming you had a touch-tone phone and not a rotary—to buy tickets for the next available showing. Somehow it seemed more complicated than just getting in line.

The line could even be fun. It's where you saw your friends from school and older kids who'd graduated and returned during a vacation. You flirted and fumbled through first-date conversations.

If you were older and had kids, you had to arrange for a babysitter, shell out the money to pay her, and drop her back off at the end of the night. After all the waiting and all the buildup, the movie might turn out to be awful. The reviews didn't come out until Friday morning, having been rushed into print when the critic filed at ten P.M. the night before. Unless you paid attention to news out of Venice or Sundance (and who did?), there was little by way of "buzz." There were no rogue online reviews or Rotten Tomatoes.

Nowadays, few spend fourteen dollars on a ticket for a movie that might not meet their standards or match their mood at that exact moment. Netflix delivers recommendations based on what you last watched, and YouTube knows if you like things a little sappy or a lot edgy and if you have a penchant for sad stories about injured wildlife. It observes which videos you watch and for how long, what you share and comment on, and enters it all into its all-seeing, AI-enhanced algorithm. Along the way it has learned your gender, where you live, and the device you're watching on.

A two-hour movie that comes out in a theater and can

be watched only once and which you may not like at all but cannot click away from, in which you have to worry about the idiots arguing during the climax or constantly checking their phones, is no comparison to the immediacy, privacy, and flexibility of whatever you can watch on-screen at home. It's hard to argue with the ability to pause when you need go to the bathroom.

Oh, but the hassle was worth it! Pause a moment to lament the passing of the legendary Ziegfeld Theatre in Manhattan, with its one magisterial screen, occasionally showing a film of apposite glory, like a revival of *Lawrence of Arabia* in an anniversary print. Even to walk by its red carpets when it was gussied up for a New York premiere and gawk at the lucky ones who were headed inside. You didn't dare walk out in the middle of a show at the Ziegfeld for a pee. It was worth it when you and a group of friends saw what would go on to become a big hit on opening night, knowing right away that you were experiencing something together that would soon sweep the nation. It was worth it to watch a film with a crowd, sensing their fear and sharing their gasps and enjoying the camaraderie of community and the human gratification of being part of a room full of laughter or tears.

LOSING THE INSTRUCTION MANUAL

Nobody misses the instruction manual that nobody could ever find because you no longer have any need for it whatsoever. Those saddle-stitched pamphlets poorly translated into Japanese, Chinese, German, French, Spanish, and, on occasion, decipherable English, if even included with your purchase, can go straight in the trash. Instead, you go online to image-search a detailed replica set or watch a how-to video on YouTube or endure a live chat with a technician on the manufacturer's website. You can pop into a discussion among techies that solves problems the instruction manual never even foresaw, or just say to hell with it and hire a TaskRabbit to put together that Ikea daybed for you.

THE BLIND DATE

A blind date was called that for a reason. You had no idea what you were getting into and not a clue what she looked like beyond what you'd been told about her hair and what color sweater she'd be wearing that night. Maybe you knew a fact or two, like where she went to college and that she was in advertising and was unusually tall, or that she'd just broken up with a longtime boyfriend.

With this scant information, you'd walk into the bar, peer around, not even sure whether the person you were meeting was there or that you would recognize each other, worried that you got the place wrong or that the other person had bailed at the last minute. You'd do that awkward dance—"Excuse me, are you waiting for someone?"— table by table. It was exciting and romantic and terrifying.

You never have to fly blind like that again because you suss all this out beforehand. Even if there's a chance you might get caught in the process, while viewing an Instagram story, for example, or checking out a LinkedIn profile, you will still snoop around online before saying yes to Thursday night. First impressions never take place at the candlelit table in the back of a restaurant. They've already happened.

"Thanks to Tinder, texting, and social media in general you're expected to know each other before you go on a date, which puts even more expectations on the date itself," reads one recent Reddit thread, neatly summing up the ruthless new efficiency behind first dates. But therein lies a loss: "I miss getting to know people in person. Even if I can ask the same questions over text the subtle facial and body cues aren't there and what might have been a great connection gets missed . . . because the vast majority of the factors that go into attraction are being ruled out with all emphasis remaining on how good people are at communicating, or manipulating, verbally."

It's a two-way street. Like anyone else with the remotest online presence, you are the sum of your digital self, tallied up by a potential partner the same way corporate data collectors peruse and categorize your personal life for profit. First impressions for everything—not just dates but also meetings, auditions, classes, interviews—take place in the cloud before they transpire anywhere down on earth. The hiring manager will delve into your social media feed, interrogate every gap in your LinkedIn, and sift through your contacts. According to a 2017 survey, 70 percent of employers do a thorough social media screening before bringing a candidate in for an interview. They know who you are well before that first encounter. Your date probably worked out the odds of whether there'll be a second date before you walked in the door; that is, if she agreed to go out with you in the first place, knowing all the details about your most recent breakup from your ex. (His version.)

Well, thank goodness? At least in part, because let's face it: Blind dates were often torture. When the person meeting you at the Italian place was sweaty, boorish, and used his napkin as a tissue, you'd feel the keen loss of an evening better spent with a book or TV show, and, possibly, betrayed by whoever set you up in the first place. Was her estimation of your dating potential that low? The only thing to do was to plot your early escape and, once home, process both the guilt over rejecting your prospective date and the lingering fear that the person you were on a date with had likewise chosen to reject you. The Internet can, at least, improve the odds. It can stop many of those dates from happening at all.

89

THE ENCYCLOPEDIA

In my childhood view of the world, kids were either born into a fun-loving, full-color *World Book Encyclopedia* family or consigned to a boring, beige *Encyclopedia Britannica* family like mine. While some who grew up in an *Encyclopedia Britannica* family may have felt morally and intellectually superior to their *World Book* counterparts, in my view, the lucky kids and the good parents were in the *World Book* families, where people appreciated that kids enjoyed pictures and text that didn't completely dull the senses.

But you were stuck with the hand you were dealt, and if you wanted to find the answer to something, it was to the encyclopedia you went, even if, like me, all you had on hand was the *Britannica*. The other option was to trek to the reference room of the library where a pristine set of *World Book*s were available for consultation. And if the answer you needed for your social studies report wasn't in there, it was straight to the dread microfiche, where no matter how you inserted the tape off the long plastic tubes, the images showed up backward and upside down. (What was the difference between microfiche and microfilm? That required a degree in library science to answer.)

Now those answers are always in high-definition full color. You can choose from one of the more than one billion videos on YouTube with "how to" in the title. You can watch a "learning video" on YouTube, as 70 percent of millennials now do as a matter of course. You can type in the first few words of your question and see your search auto-populate not only with your question but with the three follow-up questions you were planning to ask as well. You can choose whichever encyclopedia you please, at your fingertips, eternally updated, not just Wikipedia but everywhere else online, and if the facts aren't necessarily quite right, at least everyone else is riding on the same misinformation.

The 2010 version of the fifteenth edition of the *Encyclopedia Britannica,* which included thirty-two volumes and 32,640 pages in total, was the very last printed on paper. You can't be an *Encyclopedia Britannica* family if you wanted to, and who would? The Internet *is* the encyclopedia, and it's way more visual and interactive than the *World Book* ever was.

90

THE NEW KID

That poor new kid. He'd show up one day, sometimes not even on the first day of school, presenting a total cipher for the rest of the class to stare at and solve, no indication whether he'd been admired or scorned in his former town, whether he was someone to get to know or someone to shy away from. He could be the kid whose parent had died or the kid who ruled his old school. He could wind up being your best friend or your tormentor, but at this early stage, there was no saying who this kid might be.

At some point in life, everyone got their chance to be that new kid, even if the opportunity didn't arise until high school was over. Come graduation, a football player could dye his hair blue and come out of the closet, and soon after declare a semiotics major without so much as a backward glance at the former classmates who would have called him out on his sudden metamorphosis. He could work out the kinks of this new identity over the summer in total privacy and then introduce his new self at freshman orientation three states away, by which time most people back home would have forgotten who he used to be.

It was so freeing! A college girl could decide that things would be different when she returned from junior year abroad; she could transfer schools or, at a large school, find a new roommate, change her major, and stop parking herself by the keg at frat parties. A new graduate might decide that life would be better in New York than it had been in Cleveland, and he was never going back. At your next job, you'd build a fresh reputation; people wouldn't think of you as the person who spent four years as an assistant. Your new girlfriend didn't need to know about the last one. You could even take drastic steps to bury the past, like changing your name, unlisting your number, and choosing not to forward your mail. It wasn't impossible to shed a past version of yourself, *Gone Girl*–style but without the sadism or murder, and start all over again.

Not anymore. Even kids who move in sixth grade don't get to be the new kid because our social lives no longer depend on our geographic lives; they move with us regardless of where we go. The other kids can see that nobody's following you on Instagram, and those other kids follow you to your new town. There's no such thing as turning over a new leaf or total reinvention when your twelve-year-old self is sewn into the fabric of the web. "The whole system is giving very ambitious people much less chance to reinvent themselves," says Jaron Lanier, author of *You Are Not a Gadget*. Who would Bob Dylan have been, he wondered, if Robert Zimmerman were there with him the whole time?

In the Before Times, unless you were famous or had written a memoir, your childhood—and perhaps most important, your adolescence—was forgotten, a vestige of a former self that might be encountered only during a chance run-in with a hometown acquaintance. You could rest assured that nobody in your office knew that their current well-dressed power boss—admired, respected, slightly feared—was the kid who was perennially picked last in gym class.

But those childhoods no longer go away. If your mom blogged about your residual bed-wetting at age ten, it will stick to the Internet like superglue. You cannot, no matter how many times you try, remove an unflattering link off your Wikipedia page without some anonymous editor insisting it back. Even low-lying adolescent infractions like suggestive posing and graphic language gain potency when addressed to hundreds of thousands of viewers, and they have the endurance of a tattoo. Those guilty of a more serious trespass may never live it down.

In its early days, the Internet offered ways for kids to try out new selves—to play with fantasy versions of themselves in online gaming, to experiment with gender identity in an anonymous forum, to invent an avatar and see if it might, in fact, be closer to one's "real" self than the person everyone assumed you to be. But the Internet that emerged later on—data-driven, shared, permanent, profit-driven—quashed those earlier freedoms. Now a teenager from a religious family in rural Indiana will be discovered if he explores his sexuality online and may suffer appalling consequences. It seems harder to be a kid these days, and, later, harder to let that unhappy kid go.

91

THE VIEW

Here's what you're supposed to do when you arrive at your destination: Take a deep breath, then display total surprise and awe and delight in what lies before you. Open your arms wide like you're only just now noticing this stunning panorama, and, most important, be sure to immortalize the moment. Point your phone (held above, chin down, don't forget to capture the sweeping background and take several in case your eyes go weird), and you've got it. You've taken in the view.

In truth, you've already scoped out this view on multiple platforms, photos occasionally featuring Justin Bieber inexplicably posed in the foreground, and you've read the reviews and analyzed the starred ratings, and let's face it, you chose to visit this particular Icelandic beach in the first place because you *knew* what it would look like, even though you hate Justin Bieber and couldn't care less what he enjoys in a beach setting. But here you are, allowing what you see online to determine what you see in real life. You may not have come to Iceland in the first place had it not been for its social media stardom, with its live cams of geothermic pools and 360-degree tours of lava beaches. How, really, did you get to where you are?

Before social media, there was Fodor's. There would have been a few small, cheaply produced photographs interspersed in the text, and that photo might even bear a resemblance to what you saw in real life. But you would wait until the plane landed to be dazzled, your chances increased because you hadn't already seen an optimized panorama with a supersaturated beach filter.

Remember what it was like when every trip was a series of things you'd never seen before, what it was like to see things only firsthand? Remember the offline definition of unfiltered? Recently, after an outdoor dinner one night with a group of friends, I looked up and saw a faint reddish dot overhead. "I think that's Mars!" I said with a hint of pride and no small delight. Before I could search for the moon or other planets, one of the friends had whipped out her phone, pointed it at the dot, and tapped her Night Sky app. "Yup," she said in a resolute manner, as if confirming the diagnosis of a skin condition. "That's definitely Mars and over there is Saturn." We all turned away from the sky to peer into her phone.

Sometimes, that online view is all you get, and it's a whole lot cheaper than an international flight; you just spin that Google Earth and take in the views. The sun is always shining, and the image definition is spectacular. But as with so many other things, you tend to lose the big picture when you're seeing it only on a small screen.

92

SCRABBLE TILES

I can't get anyone to play Scrabble, or what I like to call "real Scrabble," with me—the kind with a gameboard and lettered tiles, no matter whether they're the immaculately buffed wooden ones or the cheaper plastic kind. Either way, they offer a delicious tactile smoothness, filling the little black drawstring bag and slipping between your fingers as you withdraw what you hope will be the perfect set of seven. You'd place them in your display rack and guard them like you were holding down a trench line.

With real Scrabble, you can't test out a word first with a built-in dictionary. You can lose your turn for trying to play a nonexistent word. There's no genius teacher pointing out how many points you could've gotten had you played your very best.

With online Scrabble, you never inadvertently show your hand to the person sitting next to you. You don't have to argue over whether your brother peeped at the letters before picking them out of the bag or "accidentally" took four tiles instead of three, or has been playing all along with eight rather than seven. You don't have to count up the tiles and compare the totals to the guide on the side of the board to make sure one isn't marooned under the sofa. You never lose a tile. You don't need tiles anymore.

You don't have to persuade anyone to play Scrabble

with you because you can play anyway, whether it's with a stranger from across the vast unknown Internet or with a friend who lives across the country. Most people, if they even still have a basis for comparison, find Scrabble to be much better this way. The rest of us play Spelling Bee now instead.

93

HUMILITY

"Stop showing off!" we were told. Don't toot your own horn. Me, me, me, all the time! You don't want to sound full of yourself. You'll come across as conceited. Don't rub it in. Try not to make other people feel bad. These harping admonitions sound like the stern entreaties of a sixteenth-century Puritan, switch at the ready, but they were par for the course in the parenting handbook as recently as 1978.

It's difficult now to imagine that pride was—and still is, biblically speaking—a sin, because we are all *so proud.* We are proud of our son's winning goal and we're a proud supporter of NPR. We are proud to have voted—take a sticker and be sure to show it off online. We are eager to tell everyone about these points of pride and to be recognized for them with a like and a star. We are proud to take part in today's social media social justice movement and wave the right signal. We look for the sweet and safe spot between the proud and the fake and the dread humblebrag so as to please our allies even as we simultaneously make them feel a teensy bit worse about themselves. Being proud (or showing off or bragging, as it was once occasionally known) isn't something we do in front of a small group of friends or colleagues anymore; it's something belted out to the entire Internet. Four in ten teenagers say they feel pressure to post *only* content that makes them look good to others or share things that will get a lot of likes or comments. The more you get, the better you are, as long as you don't look like you're trying too hard.

The constant need to show off your best online angle means constructing a façade that's hard for any fallible human being to maintain. But retaining that sense of authenticity is particularly tough on those who've committed to making a living off it—the social media stars, the influencers, the online thought leaders. What may begin as a passion project can feel like a trap when it must bend to the whims of an audience. For those who depend on YouTube for income, catering to the algorithm with ever more pleasing posts can be about making a living, which ups the incentive to stay on top. On TikTok, same thing. Maria Shabalin, a TikTok influencer who had two million fans by the time she'd graduated eighth grade, told *The New York Times,* "There was a part of the app, like a chart that would rank the influencers. And I remember checking it and thinking: 'Why am I not on the top? What do I have to do to get to the top?'" Somehow, the fact that pushing your way to the top means pushing others out of the way or somehow making them feel worse or "less than"— one of the main reasons our parents taught us not to brag in the first place—gets lost. One person's "feel good" moment is another person's "feel bad," and it all takes place not in a schoolyard or an office park, but everywhere.

It's easy to write this off as a problem for the Internet famous, but even us regular folk can have a hard time showing only our best side on a playing field that somehow always turns our personal wins into another person's implied fail: A job promotion. (Show-off.) A photograph of your child. (Cute.) A bad hair day. (The good Meg Ryan vibe.) Your new coffee table. (That you can afford.) Your extended family trip. (Not everyone gets along with the in-laws.) Your much-needed vacation to Croatia. (We can't all afford Europe.) Everything that makes you feel good can end up making another person feel bad, and you have no idea it's happening because the only signal you're getting is an absence of a signal, or a faded signal (perhaps a mere like rather than a love).

Charity, that supposed selfless act, can feel performa-tive when our benevolent leanings and GoFundMe contri-butions, our support for breast cancer awareness and our birthday donations on Facebook, and don't forget the seven P.M. cheer for emergency workers, are all on display. What would have seemed like a default position—doing nothing—now means you don't care. You are not an ally or a supporter or a remotely good person. Better to show (and show off) otherwise next time. Perhaps in what's become such a poisoned atmosphere, the online arena of endless and amplified self-aggrandizement and winner-takes-all competition, we are especially eager to prove that at the same time, we still care. We certainly care what others think.

But it can all come across as some kind of contest at life. To show something online is in some way or another to show it off. Was the death knell of Beto O'Rourke's pres-idential bid the posting of his routine dental cleaning on social media, a ghoulish public invitation into the candi-date's mouth, dank molars and all? Did he think he was so special that we'd want to see *that*? Or that he was so normal that he would post it just like he'd post dinner with the fam? It's not always easy to figure out intention with the

Internet's built-in amplifier. In the end, the Internet may succeed in turning us all into reality TV characters—highlighting our best attributes, mugging with exaggeration to be certain the "audience" catches on. Were we always this way, just without the means to telegraph it, or does the Internet turn us all into show-offs?

94

CLIFFSNOTES

The seasoned teacher always knew what was in the CliffsNotes, whether it was *Animal Farm* or the *Aeneid,* because every class might contain a cheat or two, and a deep familiarity with what was in the CliffsNotes was the most likely way to nail them. This didn't stop the desperate and misguided student from heading to the local stationery store for that spinning rack of shame, where reams of yellow booklets with their urgent hazard stripes and black ink drawings thwarted anything approaching a subtle purchase.

These days, a kid can't get busted buying CliffsNotes, because the CliffsNotes are online where no one can get caught reading them, not that a kid would bother. Why would they when they can google, skim, share ("collaborate"), search keywords, sniff out the essentials, copying and pasting and lightly altering to cover their tracks. The entire Internet is CliffsNotes.

And the Internet comes with a suite of alternatives. Why search for primary resources when someone else has already done the work for you and compiled it on a blog? With a little money, you can track down an impoverished grad student to write the paper for you.

Administrators and teachers no longer assume that students do the assigned reading at all but start instead with the assumption that every child is a potential cheat. Student work is routinely sifted by an anti-plagiarism program like Turnitin or Copyscape. But kids today know just how to sneak a purloined paper past the anti-plagiarism programs. Why shouldn't they? When schools don't operate by an honor system or high expectations, they don't offer children the basic respect of assumed innocence and good faith. Instead of hoping to dazzle his teacher with his writing or at least impress her with his ideas, the honest and hardworking kid is left simply hoping the teacher will believe he wrote it himself.

95

A PARENT'S UNDIVIDED ATTENTION

B esotted adoration is the birthright of every newborn, and parents are willing participants in this devotion. Any new parent just wants to soak up the deliciousness of their baby gazing upon them, the source and bearer of all love. Those silent exchanges, followed by the mirrored cooing, parent echoing child, carry an intensity unlike any other relationship, and the first time you feel it, the years of bewilderment you felt as a nonparent watching those wacky infatuated parents grin frantically in front of a bassinet evaporates. This profound human-to-human exchange is wordless, but as soon as the baby has words, the parent hangs on to each and every one of those early, inept articulations. A combination of pattering and continual eye contact carries on like a mutual love affair bordering on obsession. People just cannot stop looking at their babies.

Except, as it turns out, they can and they have. These days they "use" the minutes they used to "lose" pushing the carriage and babbling at the baby below, mindlessly describing the scenery or plans for the morning, knowing the baby couldn't possibly understand but maybe enjoyed the one-way convo anyway. With a phone perched on the stroller's overhead flap (multiple models now come equipped with a special holder to make this easier), scrolling or chatting with a friend or listening to a podcast fills up this time instead. There's a lot that can get done in one of those rare moments when you don't *have* to do something or be operating at full capacity, and any experienced parent knows even half-empty time is in short supply.

The Internet is full of photos shaming parents for their neglectful phone parenting at the playground, but they may in fact be parenting on their phones. (Also, those photos are taken on phones. Sometimes by other parents.) They may be checking the weather to make sure those worrisome clouds overhead don't portend a rained-out afternoon, or ordering a grocery delivery for the toddler's dinner that night. They may be texting with another child's father to arrange a playdate, or any one of the myriad tasks of daily parenthood that are more easily accomplished online. They may be, in many ways, using online tools to be the best parent possible.

Still, the effect is to remove a parent from the immediacy and totality of the sounds and sights of the human being crawling in front of him. The parent who keeps looking down at the phone, while murmuring "Oh, wow" and "Great, sweetie!" signals to a toddler, "I'm not actually talking to you right now. I'm talking to someone else. I'm looking at something else, even as I glance intermittently your way. It kind of looks like I hear you but it's just pretend." Children can tell when we're not attending to them with the little indicators of appreciation and interaction—the nods, the smiles, the matching of the mood. They know from experience that kind of total attention and can recognize when they've lost it. They are watching, and they are learning.

By the time kids are teenagers, they've definitely gotten the message.

96

TOUCH-TYPING

If your ambitions in life included functional adulthood, you had to learn how to type just like you had to learn how to tie your shoelaces. That meant going through one of those grim "touch-typing is easy" workbooks at home or sitting through a required typing class in seventh grade, banging out repetitive exercises in unison, possibly the most boring class in all of junior high. But typing class was like shop—because who shouldn't know how to hold a hammer?—one of the less taxing requirements on the road to adulthood, and, at worst, an easy B.

It turns out not to have been true. Look around and you'll find plenty of adults hunting and pecking and over-taxing their worn-out thumbs. New grown-ups don't know how to type.

Anyone who has mastered the QWERTY keyboard knows just how excruciating it is to watch someone who doesn't know how to type, like watching the tail of a rabbit trailing sixty feet behind its nose, humans moving at a puzzlingly slow rate against the warp speed of a 5G network. You can practically see the carpal tunnel develop in the hunt-and-pecker's tendons as they grope for the shift key. On the phone for twenty minutes trying to make a dermatologist appointment, you can practically hear the other person searching for number keys as they pant,

"Hold on, just a moment" and a tap tap-tap-tap, and a "Just waiting for this page to load" and an "I'm not in that window yet, you'll have to wait" and an "Our system just went down." If only someone would simply grab a pen and jot it all down.

You would think that with the Chromebooks and iPads and twenty-first-century skills, kids would be wonderful typists—*not that word, oldster!*—keyboardists, by now. But it turns out, the kids who can't handwrite in fourth grade also can't touch-type when they get to middle school. Just as schools ignore cursive, they have abandoned typing in their rush to get kids onscreen. At best, students are given a password to an online touch-typing program and expected to get up to speed on their own rather than wasting curriculum time with a structured and graded class. Most kids abandon these ineffective apps quickly or don't bother in the first place. Let loose in a field of keys, they will hunt and peck for years, developing bad habits that then become hard to undo.

When we lose touch-typing, we lose the ability to write freely without worrying where the "M" is. We lose the ability to listen and type at the same time, and to look in someone's eyes while recording their speech verbatim and not have to think about needing a capital letter because that maneuver is hardwired in. Touch-typing is like riding a bike, a kind of cognitive automaticity; once you know how, you can do it without thinking about it, freeing your mind to think about ideas, sentence structure, language, rhythm and flow. You write faster and you write better.

In lieu of developing these lifelong skills, kids will develop repetitive stress injuries from the incorrect positioning and posture they've adopted to compensate. Sure, this probably won't happen for years and is therefore not the problem of the schools that failed to instruct them in the first place. By then, those kids will probably already be in physical therapy for neck strain.

97

PHOTO ALBUMS

Your old-world albums may emerge from the bottom of the cabinet they've resided in for years only on rare occasion, but it's comforting to know that they're there. You've got your father's faux leather albums, too, and possibly those of a grandparent, and even if you're not entirely sure who half those people in there are, the full sweep of your greater history feels like it belongs in your hands. One day you'll go through them. Until then, they're safe, along with your children's baby books with their precious sealed packets of hair.

For one pre-smartphone moment, it seemed like photo albums would maintain their hold on a post-Internet world. Stationery stores abounded with spiffy improvements over the adhesive pages of the seventies, the ones that yellowed and lost their stick, the ones with pockets that never fit all the photos in your arsenal and you had to keep flipping the album around in your lap to look at the vertical shots along with the horizontal. Upscale stores offered low-tech improvements such as albums with matte pages and adhesive corner brackets, and covers in colors other than royal blue and burgundy. Scrapbooking became a thing. Everyone seemed to be storing images of their beloveds in bespoke fashion.

Then along came the iPhone. With its astounding little

camera and the cloud set up to store the vast quantity of photos we all began taking, this handy little device gave no reason to limit yourself to a few photo albums, no matter how fancy. You didn't have to spend time and money printing out photos at all. Instead, you could upload them to Apple and Google and Amazon and they would do the sorting and containing. This these companies do happily, because to them, each photo is a data point, helping improve their facial recognition technology, enhance their customer profiles, identify influencer relationships between consumers, and locate trends. We still keep our photos—we just don't keep them to ourselves.

Any cloud album can be hacked and pictures of our naked children splashing in the tub or running into ocean waves swifted off to the Dark Web. We generally don't think about where our photos end up, because it's so convenient and gratifying to scroll through the theme albums the iPhone puts together for you, the memories resurfaced. Those smiles, those forgotten small moments. You can look at them anytime, and you do—and perhaps others do, too.

98

BLOCKING THINGS OUT

C ertain things we'd prefer not to see. Our photos, so cheap and abundant, are just as likely to memorialize moments to forget as ones to look back on with fondness. You can relive every traumatic micro-moment of the last decade just by scrolling into your cache or into albums shared among friends and family members. Something is bound to make you feel bad now, even if it made you feel good at the time; perhaps you just miss that younger you. But nobody bothers to delete photos posted long ago, no matter how painful, perhaps because they don't quite feel "real" in the way a stiff-backed Polaroid did.

Before the Internet, objects imbued with the aftermath of spurned love, stupid mistakes, and twentysomething regrets were chucked into the abyss or carted off to Goodwill, and nobody took a picture of them and then posted them for sale on eBay. Other people didn't parade sources of your pain around for you to see and in ways that make them hard to unsee. But pictures taken by someone else and posted to their Facebook feed stay put and we don't have the power to remove them; we can't refuse someone else the right to display what they like. So while it's true that you can tell your story to massive numbers of people in a way you never could before the Internet, so can everyone else, and they can tell *yours*—or their own version of it.

In Ted Chiang's short story "The Truth of Fact, The Truth of Feeling," people with implanted video recordings of all their experiences are able to call up specific memories on demand, as if they had built-in search engines in their brains. In this way, the "I never said that!" marital dispute can be verified or refuted; fuzzy childhood memories can be retrieved in an instant. You can always find out what happened, depriving people of the ability to revise a painful experience into a more easily reconciled memory or to lose it altogether. In certain instances, the result is clarity, but it can also cause an almost unspeakable pain. One doesn't always benefit from being confronted with the unfiltered realities of one's past. A similar concept was explored in "The Entire History of You" episode of the TV series *Black Mirror,* in which a husband sifts through his wife's recent past to sniff out her infidelities. Being able to excavate your entire past at any given moment is almost the same as being forced to do so; it's nearly impossible to look away.

Most adults don't vividly recall every instance of embarrassment, shame, humiliation, loneliness, and fear from our pasts for a reason: Our memories are *supposed* to blur them out to help us function. The pangs of childbirth fade over time; the blackest stages of the grieving process after a death eventually lift. Human beings generally favor happy memories over sad ones, a built-in coping mechanism that aids in our psychological survival. We discard difficult memories because it's in our best interest. That's how people get by.

99

SOCIAL CUES

M uch of the work of early childhood is social development, the process by which a small child learns to
think beyond the circumference of his own feelings and
take other peoples' feelings into account. It's not easy for
any of us. But most of this we pick up along the journey to
adulthood by perceiving and absorbing the way other people act, with the help of an increasingly recognizable array
of social cues: the nods, smiles, grimaces, averted eyes,
tap-tapping toes, and hunched shoulders.

Over time, people learn to sort out the positive from the
negative. Among the many signals that point us down the
path to regret, there's the wan praise offered by the mother-
in-law over a new haircut and the way guests prod the
grilled salmon around their plates, declining seconds. It's
in the faint applause at the end of the piano recital or in
the ambiguous murmuring noise when someone asks
whether a new jumpsuit is flattering. Most people can
sense through a combination of tone, facial expression,

body language, and that ineffable something in the air, how people *really* feel, whether it's about a new boyfriend or a speech or a prototype at work—no matter what they put into words. We can tell when people don't love it. We realize pretty fast that people aren't that into the long story you're excitedly telling. We read the room.

Those signs are what let us know when we screw something up. You can tell in a meeting if people didn't appreciate your catty aside or at a party when people think your amusing anecdote is in fact obnoxious. You Have Made a Bad Move. You know to adjust—to tone it down or offer a self-deprecating laugh or to just—now, please—pass the mic.

But when we talk with our thumbs instead of our voices, the telltale signals of boredom, annoyance, hurt, and delight are leached out of the conversation. Even though it sometimes seems so encouraging! You get a "yessssss" and a smattering of likes—a "wow" for the photo of the grilled salmon and a heart or clapping hands for the jumpsuit selfie, an "LOL!" for the impolitic put-down of a senatorial candidate—any one of which is enough to inspire you to take it one step further, unaware that in another corner of the Internet, an offshoot group is groaning over what you just "said." You can dig a hole you don't realize you're in until it's too late. Even with a full range of emojis, online dialogue gets flattened into smiley faces or Japanese ogres, up votes and down votes, all the nuance rubbed out. In a group text, you can't tell if someone is quiet because they're upset; perhaps they're just offline or in another window. It's hard to read the room when you're not physically *in* the room or to gauge another person's facial expression when you're texting.

At some point you might worry that you've become
That Person, the one other people discuss elsewhere online or even offline in unflattering ways. There's that person who reveals too much about her depression or displays
too many awkward-cute pictures of her fourteen-year-old.
The person who complains about her previous job in ways
that may not bode well for her future employment. You
want to say, "Please don't do that," but instead you heart
only one of her three posts, hoping she will read the online
tea leaves. Meanwhile, so many other "friends" online—
count them!—seem to be saying precisely the opposite.
How the hell is she supposed to figure out what it all
means? Only offline do you find out what people truly
think.

CLOSURE

You could count on friends and family to offer the same set of reassurances after a rough experience: "This will all feel very different in the morning/next week/next year/with time." "Don't worry—nobody will remember." "You're the only one thinking about it." Of course you wanted to believe these platitudes, and most of the time you could because they had the benefit of being true. Mistakes were made and bad things happened, people got hurt (especially you) and then people forgot (even you) and moved on. People got pretty good at putting things so deep in the past that when confronted with one of their own long-ago misdeeds, most could persuade themselves they'd had nothing to do with it.

It may now be time to close the book on the concept of closing the book. Because nothing—not even the tiniest and most insignificant thing—ever ends online, just as the Internet itself never ends. No one forgets and no one carries on as if nothing happened—least of all you, or so it may feel—each of us lugging along the most tormented episodes of our past into the future in our own special torturous way. (Personalization!)

In lieu of a paper trail, we leave multiple digital trails: fights conducted over long strings of text that can be resurfaced during a divorce proceeding; an exchange of confidential personnel information between colleagues that somehow gets out; sexts between otherwise married lovers; that photo. Follow the traces of any one of these and you find yourself clinging against your better instincts to minor incidents, bitter mistakes, and stupid embarrassments for far too long, reliving them in an endless loop of stress, temporary recovery, relapse, and PTSD. Deeply painful episodes that used to transform over time into sepia images that felt like something you once read about happening to other people never make that transition.

Closure doesn't exist in this timeless new world, because even if you choose to shut a door firmly behind you and manage not to pry it open despite the ease with which you can do so at any moment, others online—some of whom you know, some of whom you don't—will do it for you, scanning photos that were taken of you during an earlier lifetime, and resurfacing posts that were captured before you could delete them, offering them new life in the very sticky World Wide Web for whatever reasons of their own. You may just be an incidental figure in *their* story— photographed with your arms around an abusive ex in a group shot they surface to commemorate their thirtieth wedding anniversary. *Congratulations!!*

It's exhausting.

We hold on to the illusion that the cloud is ephemeral and that things that are "online only" somehow don't count, but deep down we know that all these things leave a permanent imprint. Somewhere, always, there are pieces of you out there stored in a cache, caught on a surreptitious video, something that you cannot retrieve from someone else's hard drive, flung out there like one of those jelly spiders handed out at the pediatric dentist's office that then sticks to the wall, leaving an indelible blue gooey smear in its wake.

The Internet is unforgiving and unforgetting about even the most minor gaffe, the kind of thing that used to blow over by morning. Now, the mistake lasts forever, and each stranger who comes across it anew has no idea what kind of remorse and rehabilitation took place in the wake of the incident, which may in fact have occurred months or even years before their own first encounter with it. For them it is a problem that exists in the online present. It informs their opinion of who you are in the now.

Take a stupid drunken college evening. Even if the two friends who were with you as you stumbled across campus clutching a bag of chili lime tortilla chips, your left breast exposed by a fallen dress strap, didn't record it, a total stranger did, and beamed it off to a few pals just for giggles. One of the recipients saved a screenshot just because. You don't know who, and you don't know why, and you don't know what he'll do with it, and maybe you won't know about it at all until eight months later, when it will float back down from the cloud in someone else's "story." There is no blissful certainty that as you sail through life committing the typical human being's battery of errors, misunderstandings, flubbed introductions, and inadvertently offensive remarks, nobody is entering them into the permanent record.

The right to be forgotten, which first surfaced in 2014, is only beginning to be recognized as a legitimate moral and legal concern. In 2016, the European Union introduced provisions for how data involving kids sixteen and under is collected and used. But nothing gives people that right in the United States. Code for America, a nonprofit organization modeled after Teach for America, offers a service called Clear My Record that can help people with criminal convictions get them reduced or expunged, making it easier for them to secure future housing and jobs. For the rest of us and our shameful things that don't quite rise to the level of crime, there's no protection. The United States remains the sole developed country without some kind of federal consumer data protection law or agency. Outside these kinds of comprehensive governmental measures, it's almost impossible to wipe an individual record clean, at least in any substantive and lasting way. Your digital footprint may as well be carved into concrete.

Even the dead hover online like phantoms, suggested to you as potential friends because their social media profiles are still active. Their pages remain frozen in time, as if the deceased has only gotten up from his chair and may return any moment now. Four years after his funeral, the algorithm will suggest that you celebrate a friendship anniversary with your dead uncle. Maybe you are happy to see him again in your feed, or maybe not just now and maybe not ever. It doesn't matter; you can't turn it off. Too many people you know will want to keep the dead alive, posting condolences and, later, memories, and still later, death anniversaries, an eternal scroll of grief. Everyone sits Shiva indefinitely and the wake goes on, and on.

Perhaps it's not possible to close the book entirely on

another human being. Lost cousins reach out courtesy of Ancestry and 23andMe, and a distant relative you cut ties with decisively decades ago DMs you on Twitter. During a late-night deep dive, you may discover your father had another family before he had yours. The face of the guy who date-raped you in college can pop up as Someone You Might Know. The racist boss from your first job will be promoted yet again on LinkedIn. People you used to scrub from your mind, the ones who could only be tracked down by spending hours searching for them in a library or by hiring a private detective, return unbidden. The natural comings and goings that used to constitute our social lives now keep coming back because we're all in touch forever.

Consider what it means to live a life without closure. True, not all of it is terrible, and some of it is lovely: heartwarming memories can be accessed at any time, giving them a longer tail and allowing you to bask again in a decade-old glow. You can call up a flattering email your supervisor sent you about your performance and reread it, without rummaging through a file cabinet. You can gaze deep into the eyes of your now twelve-year-old's baby face because it's your screensaver. You can watch a happy dance on TikTok or rewatch the final kiss scene in a favorite rom-com at the click of a mouse, and without having to sit through the entire movie. It's all happening right now. Joy is here for us, at our fingertips.

But when past, present, and future all stir together in the ether, it's harder than ever to differentiate between what's over and done with and what constitutes the present tense. Gone is a healthy form of compartmentalization. You can't tuck stuff on the Internet into a bottom drawer.

No longer in charge of our own timelines, we are trapped in the constant now, delivered thoughts, feelings, images, and ideas that might be years old. You may think yourself on a path forward, but you are never alone, and others around you may be cycling, churning, returning through parts of their pasts that are also your past, and you are thrust back and forward in time along with them. In the constant now, in the constant connected world, you cannot just slip out of touch or gain physical or emotional distance.

No wonder at the end of each day, it feels like we've lived through several days, our minds crowded with thoughts, feelings, and impressions that don't reflect the ordinary passage of twelve or fourteen hours but instead contain multitudes and layers of accumulated experience, some of it not even—by any common definition—our own, though now made part of our psychological landscape. We take it all on, often unwittingly (a thing that flashed by on TweetDeck, a meme embedded in a news story, a strangely disturbing video autoplaying on YouTube, a thing you did not want to see); these become a part of the information that your brain tries to process as it attempts to unwind before bedtime, desperately seeking an end to the swirl of images and reactions before it spirals. Just an ending, please. Like the devices we leave running all night, rarely bothering to power down, is it any wonder that it seems harder to turn our own brains off and go to sleep?

Perhaps it's we humans who have fallen behind the technology we created, we humans who find it hard to remember what we would like to remember, to hold on to it as something that belongs to us and us alone and keep it for ourselves. It's we humans who are unable to forget the things we've lost and to let them go. It's we who still wonder how to make these choices, when we still have them. The Internet, very good at its job, retains everything. Perhaps it will give us the chance to hold on to the good things, too.

ACKNOWLEDGMENTS

This book felt like it took a lifetime, and in a way it did, encompassing all of my grumpy-old-man thoughts and wary skepticism, lashed through with a contrary streak of optimism, accumulated over years of observing the culture and covering its manifestations and effects. It also felt like it took a long time because it included a year of writing on trains, and then, when the train riding ceased, writing around the edges of my days during the seven-year-long quarantine.

Thanks as ever to my agent, Lydia Wills; my how-lucky-am-I-to-have-her editor, Gillian Blake; Caroline Wray, Chris Brand, Luke Epplin, Michelle Daniel, and the entire team at Crown. Thanks to the genius that is Nishant Choksi. When I decided this book should be illustrated, he was the only name on my list. I couldn't think beyond the disappointment I would have endured if he'd said no. "These illustrations will make people think your book is fun," one of my children observed. Here's my view: These illustrations make this book. Thank you, Nishant, for saying yes.

Thanks to the incomparable Honor Jones, who got this whole thing kick-started editing my op-ed on boredom. Thanks to the poor souls who read early drafts and made clear everything that was terribly wrong: Bob Gottlieb,

Sarah Lyall, Susan Dominus, Debra Stern, and Ericka Tullis. Thank you to the many friends who got me through 2020; you know who you are, but in particular, Ericka, Sue, Sarah, Alysia Abbott, Jen Senior, and my loyal Brown crew. Thanks to those who accompanied me on my long and chilly walk-and-talks. Thanks to Cousina Kirsten and Uncle David for sharing our bubble. Thanks to Brother Rog, The Big Galoot.

Thanks most of all to my family. Throughout it all, you left me alone when I needed to be alone to work and in good company during my spare time off, giving me much needed comfort and support and distraction. Thank you for letting me kick you out and shut the door, and then welcoming me back. You made me glad to be home.

ABOUT THE AUTHOR

PAMELA PAUL is the editor of *The New York Times Book Review* and oversees book coverage at the *Times*, where she is the host of the weekly *Book Review* podcast. Her previous books include *My Life with Bob; How to Raise a Reader; By the Book; Parenting, Inc.; Pornified; The Starter Marriage and the Future of Matrimony;* and *Rectangle Time,* a book for children. Prior to joining *The New York Times,* she was a contributor to *Time* and *The Economist,* and her work has appeared in *The Atlantic, The Washington Post,* and *Vogue.*

pamelapaul.com
Twitter: @PamelaPaulNYT
Instagram: @PamelaPaul2018